NORFOLK FROM THE AIR

Speak to the earth
and it will teach you

Job XII, v.8

NORFOLK
from the air
I

Second Edition

Photography principally by
Derek A. Edwards

Edited by
Peter Wade-Martins

Field Archaeology Division
NORFOLK MUSEUMS SERVICE
Director Catherine Wilson OBE FSA FMA

Front cover Cromer
Back cover Castle Acre priory

© Copyright Norfolk Museums Service 1997
ISBN 0 903101 63 7
Second edition 1997

Designed by Richard Malt

Typeset in Palatino
Printed by Witley Press, Hunstanton, Norfolk

Contents

Foreword

When *Norfolk from the Air* was first published in 1987 it was an immediate success and quickly became the most popular publication so far produced by Norfolk Museums Service. It provided a new angle from which to view the county, and gave readers an opportunity to see the evidence for a wide range of previously unpublished archaeological sites and historic monuments.

The book went out of print all too quickly. However, now that Norfolk Museums Service has accumulated sufficient material for a second volume of pictures, the time seems right to republish the original book with minor corrections as Volume I, to be followed soon by Volume II.

The success of the original publication derived from the strong black and white images and authoritative texts, all of which have been retained. The best of the original colour material will be used again in Volume II along with much new colour and black and white photography taken in the intervening years.

The volumes will illustrate how much can be revealed by looking at the landscape from a different perspective with a critical and understanding eye. One can only wonder how much more there still remains to be discovered about Norfolk's past. I am sure that the *Norfolk from the Air* volumes will be of great interest to all those fascinated by landscapes and will be particularly valuable to students of local history. New and exciting discoveries of great interest continue to be made by the aerial photography programme organised by the Field Archaeology Division of the Norfolk Museums Service. I am sure further information about Norfolk's past will come to light in the years ahead.

Catherine Wilson,
Director
Norfolk Museums Service

Acknowledgements

While most photographs were taken by Derek Edwards for the Field Archaeology Division of the Norfolk Museums Service, others have been generously provided as follows:

Aerial Archaeology Publications 5, 14, 28, 35, 69

Ashmolean Museum, Oxford (Allen Collection) 25

Norfolk & Norwich Flying Club Ltd (formerly the Norfolk & Norwich Aero Club) 29

Royal Air Force, Crown Copyright reserved 122, p.8

Royal Commission on Historical Monuments (Crawford Collection) 22

Suffolk County Council Planning Department 16

University of Cambridge Committee for Aerial Photography 40, 42, 43, 55, 56

University of Cambridge Committee for Aerial Photography, Crown Copyright reserved 58

Permission to reproduce the map on p.12 was kindly given by Academic Press Inc. (London) Ltd.

The following authors have kindly written captions:

Brian Ayers 94-96

Michael Boon 92

Bernard Farrant 126-128

Paul Freschini 102

John Goldsmith 5, 46

Tony Gregory 16, 17

Elizabeth Griffiths 100

Frances Healy 8, 9

Michael Innes 129

Elizabeth James 85-87

June McNeil 110

Jan Murray 131

Owen Needham 130

Kenneth Penn 88, 89

Andy Reid 78, 79

Robert Rickett 27, 30, 33

Andrew Rogerson 38, 39, 44, 53, 74

Edwin Rose 29, 31, 32, 35-37, 47-49, 51, 52, 55, 60-64, 66, 68, 70, 71, 75, 80, 82-84, 97-99, 101, 103-105, 111-113

Derek Searle 132

Bob Silvester 25, 26, 59

Tony Stuart 1-4

Susanna Wade Martins 69, 76, 77, 81, 106, 107

John Wymer 6, 7, 10 11

David Yaxley 67

(The remaining captions have been compiled by the Editor.)

The air photography programme of the Field Archaeology Division has been generously supported by the Historic Buildings and Monuments Commission and previously the Department of the Environment. The Royal Commission on Historical Monuments of England has at the same time arranged the printing of all the pictures for the Division's Air Photographs Collection. Duplicate copies of all the Division's photography are held in the Air Photographs Unit within the National Monuments Record, Royal Commission on Historical Monuments of England, Swindon, and may be consulted there as well as at Gressenhall.

The compilation of this book has been very much a team effort involving many colleagues within Norfolk Museums Service who have commented on the text in its various stages. Special thanks are due to Joan Daniells who prepared the text on computer for typesetting and to Jane Everett who compiled the index.

It is also appropriate here to recognise the importance of the contribution made to the notable success of the first edition of this book by the late Richard Hubbard, at the time Publications Officer of the Norfolk Museums Service.

Peter Wade-Martins
County Field Archaeologist

Accompanying the picture titles is the grid reference indicating approximately the centre point of each picture. Guidance for the use of the grid reference system is given on Ordnance Survey maps. Comparison of the aerial photographs with OS maps will often assist the reader and a north pointer is provided to help with orientation.

*Note on access to sites
Many of the sites illustrated in this book are on private property and are **not** open to the public. Sites or areas which are open regularly to visitors are marked by an asterisk at the end of the caption.

A vertical air-photograph of Roudham taken by the R A F in 1946. An area of Breckland heath, now farmed, can be seen at the top, and at the bottom left are the earthworks of the deserted medieval village. The low-flying aircraft is about to cross the angle of the larger of two moats near the farm.

The large field on the right was part of the First World War East Harling airfield and adjacent to it is a supply dump from the last war.

Introduction

This is the first book to be published which illustrates the many and varied aspects of the Norfolk landscape as seen from the air; familiar and less familiar landmarks are viewed from a vantage point seldom accessible to most people. The selection has been made from a collection of about 70,000 aerial photographs held by the Field Archaeology Division at Gressenhall; the pictures have been chosen to provide examples of the many different types of natural and man-made features to be found in the wide variety of landscapes in the Norfolk countryside.

All but fifteen of the 153 air photographs were taken by Derek Edwards during the thirteen years prior to the publication of the first edition in 1987. The Division, as a field department of the Norfolk Museums Service, is charged with the task of recording archaeological sites and the contemporary landscape by air photography, and by ground-level surveys of archaeological sites and standing structures.

Archaeological sites and the traces of long-vanished landscapes have been disappearing at an unprecedented rate since the last war. Vertical RAF air photographs made as part of the National Air Photograph Survey of Great Britain in 1946 and 1947 have already become historic documents in their own right, no less important than the Enclosure Award maps of the last century and estate maps from the three centuries before that. Those interested in landscape history also owe an enormous debt to Professor J.K.S. St Joseph who was flying all over the country from Cambridge between 1948 and 1980. The collection of about a third of a million mostly oblique pictures (e.g. **56** & **58**) compiled by him during that time will be of untold importance to historians and archaeologists for generations to come. Many earthworks which survived in the countryside until the post-war years were recorded on these air photographs and nowhere else before the sites were destroyed in the 1950s and 1960s in the course of agricultural improvement. Similarly, photographs now assembled at Gressenhall will form an important archive for present and future research.

Readers of this book will be able to see for themselves just how significant air photography has become to the landscape historian. No written record, however precise, can provide such a comprehensive statement of any piece of landscape as an air photograph. Photography, in all its detail and subtlety, can be far more informative than mapping can ever be.

The photograph and accompanying diagram opposite show how underground features can cause visible crop marks. On the left in the diagram, a filled ditch provides a greater depth of soil, encouraging plant growth. On the right, a buried wall has the opposite effect. Both features may be visible from the air as colour differences in cereals, and these cropmarks can be enhanced by shadows when the sun is low (see, for example, **10, 22, 54**).

A considerable number of previously unknown archaeological sites have been found since the flying programme began. For instance, 196 flattened Bronze Age burial mounds or 'ring ditches' (**10 & 11**) had been recorded by 1974, and by 1986 this number had risen to 908; the figures still continue to grow, thereby transforming our understanding of the countryside in prehistory.

Of course, archaeological excavation is the only way to obtain a very detailed understanding of a site and its chronology because a camera can not see into the soil. But excavation, because it is so labour-intensive, is very expensive compared with air survey and is usually only available to record minute fragments of past landscapes. The largest excavation so far seen in the county was carried out in 1980-82 on an eleven-acre early Roman site near the Fison Way Industrial Estate at Thetford (**16 & 17**), but this was exceptional. With the resources usually available, most archaeological digs have to be relatively small. However, where the techniques of air photography can be combined with those of excavation, so that sites can be studied in their wider context, as at Spong Hill, North Elmham (**27**), the results can be impressive.

As this book shows, no archaeological air photographer can limit his work to recording just archaeological sites, while ignoring the later evidence. Burgh Castle (**20**) and Cromer Pier (**107**) are equally important as monuments to the life and times they represent. The photographic record held at Gressenhall comes right up to date with railway stations and airfields to complete the picture. Indeed, the county's Sites and Monuments Record includes some quite recent monuments.

Flicking through the book, readers may think that Norfolk is full of the earthworks and relic landscape features seen here. While it is true we still have some fine examples in the county, it is a fact that East Anglia has suffered severely from the devastating effects of large-scale arable farming since the last war, so that well-preserved monuments are now unusual. The controversy surrounding the ploughing-up of Halvergate marshes, now partially halted by payments to farmers not to disturb this grassland, is a much publicised example of the wider loss of permanent grassland, wetland, woodland and heath witnessed in the last forty years. Old meadowland, even on heavy clay soils and in river valleys, is becoming rare. While it is true that wildlife habitats are being lost, it is also a fact that archaeological monuments are being damaged or destroyed as well (e.g. **29, 42** and **43**). Nos **38** and **39** show what can happen to moated sites, a story which could be repeated hundreds of times for this and other types of sites all over the county. Earthworks often stand all too vulnerably on isolated meadows surrounded by arable fields like oases in a desert. EEC food surpluses and increased environmental

The effect of buried features on growing crops

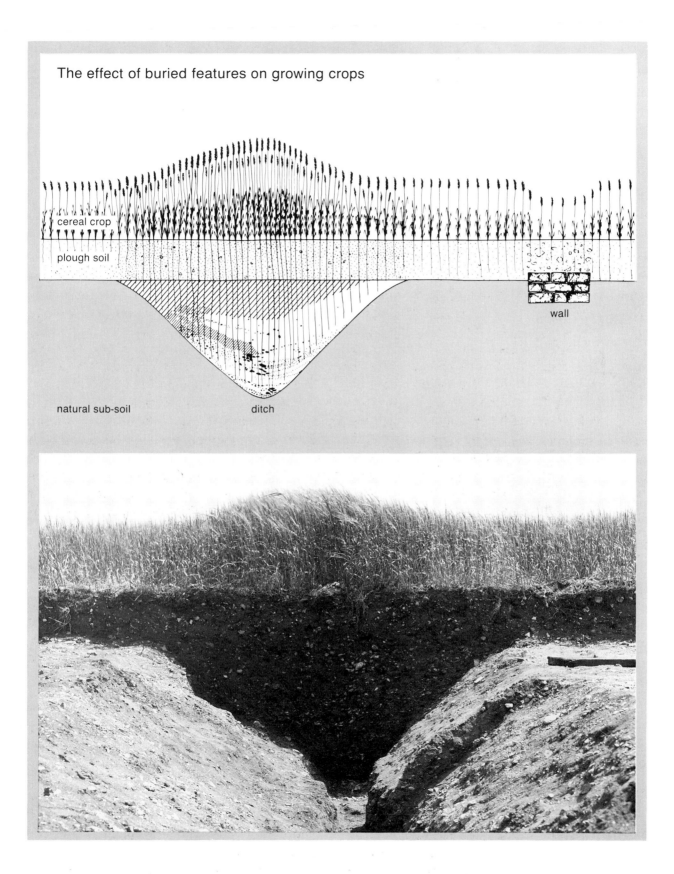

cereal crop

plough soil

wall

natural sub-soil

ditch

The hedgerow pattern of the Dickleburgh area shown
against the line of the Caistor to Scole Roman road.
(Modern parish boundaries are shown in grey)

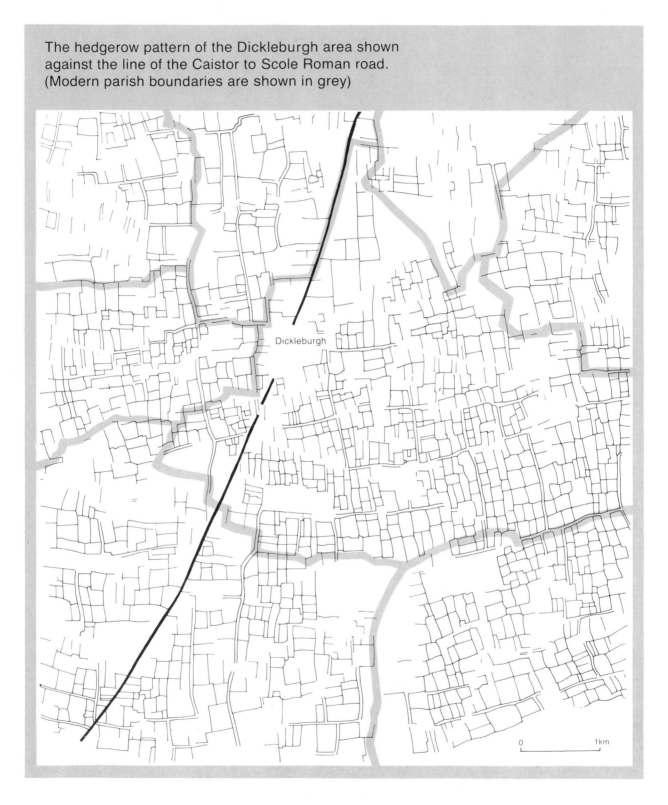

Dickleburgh

0   1km

awareness have come too late to save so much of what was worth preserving. While EEC agricultural support policies have been restructured in favour of conservation measures, there is still an urgent need to survey the remaining old grassland and to identify, record and schedule all the important ancient monuments while we still have them.

The landscape of East Anglia, as elsewhere, is the product of centuries of change, with each generation modifying, but seldom (until recently) completely sweeping away, what has gone before. The hedgerows, the lanes, the village greens, the woodland and the high streets of market towns all have their stories to tell. Landscape features of one period are inevitably influenced by the layout of what has gone before and the effect that comes after. The study of how landmarks of different dates can be related to each other is a fascinating exercise. The example in **42** is an interesting one where earthworks of a Roman settlement at Hockwold are overlaid by a medieval and later field system and are adjacent to, but separate from, the earthworks of a medieval village now partly abandoned.

It is now quite certain that settlement patterns have never been static in our region. None of the market towns of the county have Roman predecessors underlying them. The Roman capital at Caistor St Edmund (**22**) is 5km south of the centre of Norwich (**95**) and there appears to be no direct connection between them. Medieval villages are seldom apparently on the sites of their Anglo-Saxon forerunners. The village green, which used to be thought of as a typical Anglo-Saxon settlement form, is now believed in most cases to originate in the eleventh and twelfth centuries. Isolated churches (such as **51-4** & **56**) are still in the popular mind associated with the Black Death and plagues which encouraged villagers to settle on 'clean' sites elsewhere. In practice, isolated churches, and indeed isolated manor sites, are the products of a constant shift of settlement which has continued uninterrupted since prehistoric times. Churches standing alone in the countryside frequently indicate the locations of Late Saxon villages abandoned by the twelfth century. Moated sites on heavy clay soils well away from village centres (**38, 39, 47** & **74**) show where colonisation of woodland or waste land may have taken place in the Middle Ages.

However, despite this continually changing scene, there are some equally remarkable examples of continuity. One of the most exciting recent discoveries concerns the hedgerow pattern in the Dickleburgh area of south Norfolk (map on p.12). Tom Williamson at the University of East Anglia looked at the hedgerows of this area as depicted on the early nineteenth-century Tithe Award Maps. After removing those which he identified as being of recent origin, he was left with about 80% of the total; these formed a rectilinear pattern running on a north-to-south axis quite clearly *older* than the Roman road - the Pye Road - running between Caistor and Scole. So, the conclusion drawn from this is that the hedgerow pattern of the area is either early Roman or even Iron Age in origin. The significance of this for the antiquity of parts of the Norfolk landscape is quite dramatic and the implications have yet to be considered for the region as a whole. How much of the medieval landscape as it has come down to us is actually a relic of the Roman and prehistoric periods is a fascinating subject hardly yet explored.

The establishment and growth of the towns in the county is also a complex subject. Norwich (**94**) and Thetford (**84**) are both Late Saxon towns, although there are increasing hints at Norwich of a Middle Saxon forerunner lying north of the river. King's Lynn (**85**) is a Norman 'plantation' laid out as a trading centre by the bishop of Norwich in the twelfth century. Great Yarmouth grew up on its sand spit as a fishing and trading post in the tenth and eleventh centuries. The many market towns of Norfolk developed in the twelfth and thirteenth centuries providing market centres for the surrounding countryside, as to a certain extent they still do today. Along the north coast there was a whole string of small ports; while many like Cley (**89**) have lost their importance due to changing circumstances and silting estuaries, Wells (**90**) has survived both as a port and has also become a holiday centre.

Above all, Norfolk's prosperity, reflected in the frequent discovery of gold and silver objects of many periods (which are subject to Treasure Trove inquests), the very high population figures in Domesday Book, the great churches of the fifteenth century, and the size of the fortified area of Norwich - greater even than London - was based on the fertility of the soil. The economy has until recently been based on the county's agriculture and it is the wide open spaces of cereals and sugar beet which make the greatest impression even today.

Air photography, better than any other technique, documents the changing scene in the countryside, towns and cities. The building of new suburbs can completely transform an area (**102**). The construction of a fine new bridge over Breydon Water (**91**) and the East Dereham by-pass (**126 & 127**) were recorded while work was in progress. Other scenes never seem to change (**74**).

We hope that *Norfolk from the Air* will give our readers pleasure and will demonstrate the contribution air photography has and will continue to make to landscape studies. We also hope it will help people to appreciate the antiquity of the countryside and encourage those who own property to cherish and conserve the landscape for future generations to enjoy.

Peter Wade-Martins

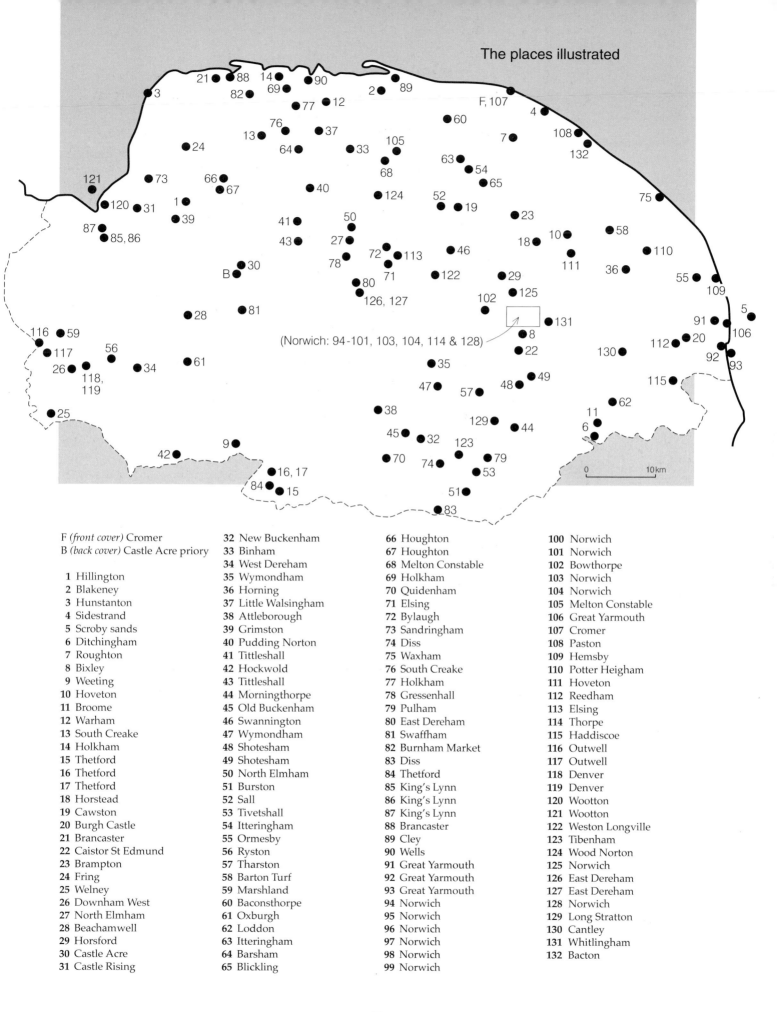

The places illustrated

(Norwich: 94-101, 103, 104, 114 & 128)

F *(front cover)* Cromer
B *(back cover)* Castle Acre priory

1 Hillington
2 Blakeney
3 Hunstanton
4 Sidestrand
5 Scroby sands
6 Ditchingham
7 Roughton
8 Bixley
9 Weeting
10 Hoveton
11 Broome
12 Warham
13 South Creake
14 Holkham
15 Thetford
16 Thetford
17 Thetford
18 Horstead
19 Cawston
20 Burgh Castle
21 Brancaster
22 Caistor St Edmund
23 Brampton
24 Fring
25 Welney
26 Downham West
27 North Elmham
28 Beachamwell
29 Horsford
30 Castle Acre
31 Castle Rising

32 New Buckenham
33 Binham
34 West Dereham
35 Wymondham
36 Horning
37 Little Walsingham
38 Attleborough
39 Grimston
40 Pudding Norton
41 Tittleshall
42 Hockwold
43 Tittleshall
44 Morningthorpe
45 Old Buckenham
46 Swannington
47 Wymondham
48 Shotesham
49 Shotesham
50 North Elmham
51 Burston
52 Sall
53 Tivetshall
54 Itteringham
55 Ormesby
56 Ryston
57 Tharston
58 Barton Turf
59 Marshland
60 Baconsthorpe
61 Oxburgh
62 Loddon
63 Itteringham
64 Barsham
65 Blickling

66 Houghton
67 Houghton
68 Melton Constable
69 Holkham
70 Quidenham
71 Elsing
72 Bylaugh
73 Sandringham
74 Diss
75 Waxham
76 South Creake
77 Holkham
78 Gressenhall
79 Pulham
80 East Dereham
81 Swaffham
82 Burnham Market
83 Diss
84 Thetford
85 King's Lynn
86 King's Lynn
87 King's Lynn
88 Brancaster
89 Cley
90 Wells
91 Great Yarmouth
92 Great Yarmouth
93 Great Yarmouth
94 Norwich
95 Norwich
96 Norwich
97 Norwich
98 Norwich
99 Norwich

100 Norwich
101 Norwich
102 Bowthorpe
103 Norwich
104 Norwich
105 Melton Constable
106 Great Yarmouth
107 Cromer
108 Paston
109 Hemsby
110 Potter Heigham
111 Hoveton
112 Reedham
113 Elsing
114 Thorpe
115 Haddiscoe
116 Outwell
117 Outwell
118 Denver
119 Denver
120 Wootton
121 Wootton
122 Weston Longville
123 Tibenham
124 Wood Norton
125 Norwich
126 East Dereham
127 East Dereham
128 Norwich
129 Long Stratton
130 Cantley
131 Whitlingham
132 Bacton

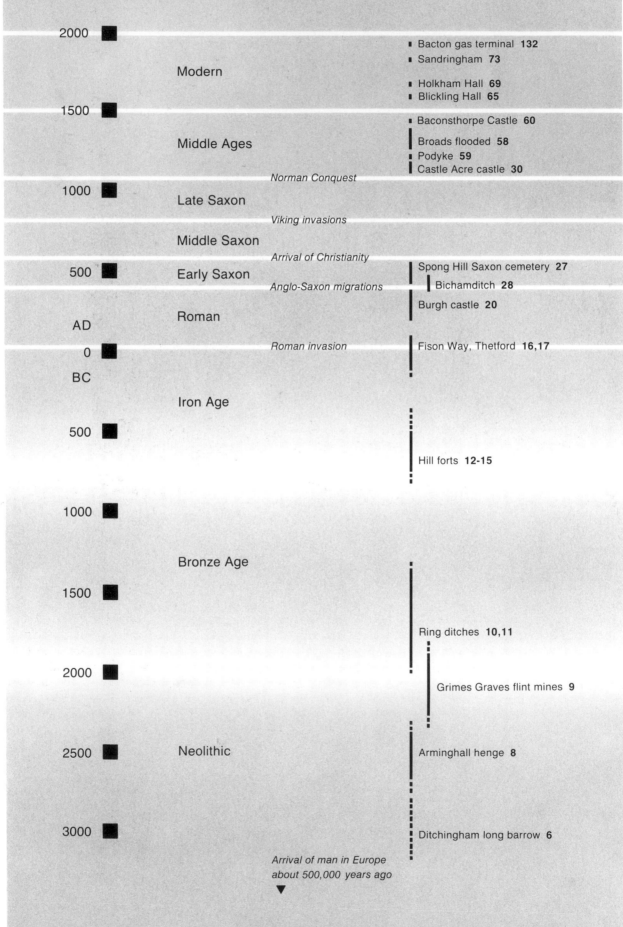

Time chart showing the dates
of a selection of sites illustrated
in the black & white photographs

2000

Modern

- Bacton gas terminal **132**
- Sandringham **73**

- Holkham Hall **69**
- Blickling Hall **65**

1500

Middle Ages

- Baconsthorpe Castle **60**
- Broads flooded **58**
- Podyke **59**
- Castle Acre castle **30**

Norman Conquest

1000

Late Saxon

Viking invasions

Middle Saxon

Arrival of Christianity

500

Early Saxon

Spong Hill Saxon cemetery **27**

Anglo-Saxon migrations

Bichamditch **28**

Roman

Burgh castle **20**

AD

0

Roman invasion

Fison Way, Thetford **16,17**

BC

Iron Age

500

Hill forts **12-15**

1000

Bronze Age

1500

Ring ditches **10,11**

2000

Grimes Graves flint mines **9**

2500

Neolithic

Arminghall henge **8**

3000

Ditchingham long barrow **6**

*Arrival of man in Europe
about 500,000 years ago*
▼

Striped patterns, Hillington

TF 746 256

The Norfolk landscape was largely shaped within the last half a million years by glaciers, rivers, coastal erosion and other natural processes. The region was invaded by glaciers on at least three occasions. The oldest and most extensive of these covered all of East Anglia, reaching as far as what is now north London, and left behind a thick blanket of boulder clays, gravels and sands when it melted. During the most recent occasion, from about 18,000 to 15,000 years ago, the ice only reached the north-west coast of Norfolk, but the area to the south was subjected to a climate of arctic severity. Under these extreme conditions, resembling those of Alaska or northern Siberia today, the subsoil was profoundly disturbed by being alternately frozen and thawed. In the west and south west of the county where chalk is exposed at the surface this repeated process resulted in chalk rubble being thrust up through the thin covering of sands and gravels to produce distinctive patterns: honeycomb networks on level ground and stripes on slopes. In this example from Hillington, West Norfolk, the stripes show up as crop-marks, with the growth of cereals reflecting the contrasting nature of the subsoil.

The deposits left by the melting glaciers commonly formed distinctive landscape features which can be recognised from their similarity to landmarks produced by glaciers at the present day. The photograph shows such a feature, called an esker, near Blakeney, north Norfolk. The unploughed gravel ridge winds between arable fields. The gravel is now commercially exploited by the quarry seen in the middle of the picture. The esker was formed where a stream deposited gravels as it escaped from a tunnel under the glacier. As the glacier melted and retreated a long ribbon of gravel was left behind.

The highly distinctive cliffs at Hunstanton in the extreme north west of the county are composed of some of the oldest rocks in Norfolk, dating from the Cretaceous Period 115 to 90 million years ago. The rocks are in layers, with the oldest at the bottom. The base of the cliff is Carstone, a rust-coloured sandstone widely used for building purposes, overlain by the thin but distinctive Red Chalk, and in turn by White Chalk which forms the top of the cliff. Under attack by the sea, accompanied by the action of rain and frost, large slabs of rock split off and accumulate at the base of the cliff, leaving a vertical face, as can be seen clearly in this photograph. However, in contrast to most other parts of the Norfolk coast (**4**), the Hunstanton cliffs are composed of rather tough rocks and coastal erosion here is relatively slow.

On top of the cliffs is the town of New Hunstanton, laid out in the 1860s by William Butterfield as a planned seaside resort for Hamon LeStrange, who lived in Hunstanton Hall (amongst the trees in the background). It was a virgin site; the old village can be seen in the distance. Only the right-hand houses in the photograph belong to the original town; most of those visible are of the 1960s.

On St Edmund's Point stands the lighthouse, built in 1830 and dismantled in 1921. It replaced a wooden predecessor of 1776 which contained the world's first parabolic reflector, made of stretched cotton. In front of it can be seen the ruins of St Edmund's Chapel, a Norman structure rebuilt in the fifteenth century.*

In marked contrast to the vertical cliffs at Hunstanton (**3**), much of the north-east coast of Norfolk is occupied by cliffs composed of soft clays, sands and gravels deposited by glaciers early in the Ice Age, about 400,000 years ago. Deposits, saturated by rainwater soaking through from above, slump down the cliff as mudflows, while large sections of the cliff slide down where rainwater has lubricated planes of weakness. The action of the sea is mainly to carry away material brought down to the beach by these processes, so that the construction of sea defences does not immediately stop coastal erosion. This photograph graphically shows the sloping cliff, eroded by the combined processes of landslipping and mudflows. Streams of freshwater can be seen flowing across the beach after escaping from either side of a mudflow.

The spread of erosion is emphasied by the fact that one slump has removed quite recent tractor marks.

Scroby sands

TG 57 08

Some 3 km out into the North Sea to the east of Great Yarmouth and parallel to the beach lies the island of Scroby. During the past four centuries this ribbon of ever-shifting sand has grounded unwary shipping and provided sanctuary for seals and sea birds. At some periods it has been almost 5 km long and higher than most tides; at other times it has been down to a football-pitch in size and usually covered at high tide.

This photograph shows the wave-rippled surface of the sand island, with the sand patterns much more complex on the landward side. There is a herd of Common Seals basking in the afternoon sunshine, their flipper marks showing as trails from the water's edge. Female Common Seals produce a single pup here in July, and a few Grey Seals produce young on the sands around Christmas time.

Common, Little and Sandwich Terns have all nested here successfully in good summers when wind and tide have combined to build the sands high, while many gull species paddle and roost at all states of the tide in all seasons.

A visit to Scroby sands is a delight in the summer months when an inshore fishing boat ferries trippers regularly from the main holiday beach at Yarmouth, out to what appears in the distance to be a long line of white foam-capped breakers.

This is a well-preserved example of a Neolithic long barrow. These earthen mounds are found over much of south east Britain, but are rare in East Anglia. Only three others survive in Norfolk, at Harpley, West Rudham and Felthorpe; others have been levelled and are only revealed by crop-marks, as at Roughton (7). They are usually flanked by ditches, or enclosed within a continuous ditch, but no trace of such can be seen here. However, the monument has never been archaeologically excavated, and filled-in ditches may still remain. The mound is 35 m long and 2 m high. Long barrows are associated with communal burial customs, but almost certainly served as well for other ritual or mystical purposes in the life of the Neolithic earliest farming communities of Britain. A Ditchingham barrow was dug into in the nineteenth century and it was possibly this one. An extended skeleton was found on the old land surface beneath. There was also charcoal in the barrow. Certainly, elaborate structures may have been incorporated in the mound, as have been found in similar monuments elsewhere in Britain, such as mortuary houses, burial chambers, cremation pyres and also dumps of household rubbish (broken pots, flint tools and animal bones). Beyond the photograph also on Broome Heath, to the south west of the long barrow, is a C-shaped enclosure just visible as an earthwork. Excavations here in 1970 and 1971 produced evidence of Neolithic settlement from four to five thousand years ago. Nearby later Bronze Age round barrows are also visible.*

Crop-marks of Neolithic Sites, Roughton

TG 220 353

The circular crop-mark reveals the remains of an enclosure *c.* 92 m in diameter, formed by the cutting of eleven ditched sections. Any banks formed by the soil thrown up from the ditches have long since been washed, thrown or ploughed back into them and no trace whatsoever is visible of this monument from the ground. Interrupted ditched enclosures are distinctive earthworks of the Neolithic period. No visible examples survive in Norfolk, but this crop-mark is almost certainly the remains of such an enclosure. Crop-marks of other possible ones are at Hainford and Marlingford.

Because of the undug sections between the ditches, these earthworks are sometimes called 'causewayed camps', but archaeologists no longer favour this, for the term 'camp' implies settlement and it is very uncertain for what purpose they were used. Suggestions have been made for their being meeting places of scattered communities, for trade, social intercourse, ceremonies and rituals. They certainly appear to have been used for one or all of these things. Similar enclosures in Wessex, where they are much more common on the chalk hills, have been excavated, but failed to produce traces of huts or any other signs of settlement. Strange assortments of dumped material including animal and human bones have been found in the ditches purposely back-filled at the time.

Interrupted ditched enclosures are often closely associated with contemporary long barrows, as at Ditchingham (6). Long barrows are sometimes enclosed by a continuous ditch and the crop-mark of such a feature shows clearly on the left of the enclosure.

Arminghall henge, Bixley

TG 239 060

The Arminghall henge was discovered from the air in 1929 by Wing Commander Insall, a pioneer of archaeological air photography. Its partial excavation by Grahame Clark in 1935 showed that the two concentric dark rings visible in the photograph represent ditches, and the central dark patches sockets for large posts. The entire monument is approximately 80 m in diameter. Earth and gravel from the ditches had been piled up to form a bank between them. This is still visible, although much-reduced by ploughing. The gap in the inner ditch led into a horseshoe-shaped setting of eight massive posts. Their sockets survived to 1.80 – 2 m deep, each cut with a slope at one side, down which the posts had been slid before being hauled upright. The discoloured soil which had gradually filled the cavities left by the decaying posts showed that they had measured up to 0.90 m in diameter. Surviving charcoal showed that they had been of oak. Each must have been the trunk of a mature tree.

Pottery from the bottom of the inner ditch and a radiocarbon determination made on charcoal from one of the central post-holes indicate that the monument was built between four and five thousand years ago. It belongs to a class of banked and ditched enclosures of apparently ceremonial function which are known as henges. Like other henges, it served as a focus around which numerous burial mounds were built. Most of these are now visible only as ring-ditches as in **10** and **11**.

The site is a scheduled ancient monument and lies under pasture on the edge of the floodplain of the river Tas. It is accessible from a public footpath which runs past its northern edge from White Horse Lane in the east to the Lakenham-Caistor St Edmund road in the west.

Grime's Graves is the site of a Neolithic flint-mining complex. It is in the guardianship of the Historic Buildings and Monuments Commission and is open to the public. Each hollow is the top of an almost completely filled-in mine shaft, originally excavated to reach a seam of particularly fine, sound flint known to the Brandon gun-flint knappers of recent times as 'floorstone'. The mined area covers at least 37 hectares, although nothing is visible on the surface in those parts of the site which have been levelled by cultivation. Recent investigations have shown that the mines were worked between 4,400 and 4,000 years ago, before metals were widely available in Britain. After the topsoil and the sand which lies beneath it were removed, the chalk was broken up with picks made from red deer antler. Where the floorstone lay close to the surface it was simply extracted by digging pits. Where it lay deeper (up to 11m at one end of the field), radiating galleries were cut from the bases of vertical shafts in order to extract as much of it as possible from each shaft. Beneath the grass, the surface between the shafts and pits is covered with the spoil cast up by the miners. Amongst the spoil-heaps, and sometimes buried beneath them, are deposits of thousands of pieces of waste flint, struck from the freshly-extracted stone. The flint was made into cutting tools, such as knives and axe heads, and probably into dressed lumps which could be taken away for further working elsewhere. The products of these mines were widely distributed over East Anglia.*

Ring-ditch cut by pipeline, Hoveton

TG 300 198

Prominent on the accompanying photograph are the crop-marks of two double-ditched concentric ring-ditches and a continuous diagonal line actually cutting through one of them. The long, straight mark is modern, caused by the cutting of a deep trench for a North Sea gas pipeline in 1970. The circular marks are the buried ditches of Early Bronze Age funerary monuments, almost certainly once burial mounds, otherwise known as 'barrows', which have since been levelled. Now, nothing whatsoever of them can be seen on the ground. Only the differential growth of crops at certain times of the year can sometimes produce these crop-marks, and even then they are virtually impossible to see or comprehend except from the air.

The ring-ditches were discovered in 1935 when they were seen from the air by Mr H.F.Low. He took photographs of them but, unfortunately these photographs were destroyed during a bombing raid in 1940, so the exact location of the barrows was lost. By 1977, the Norfolk Archaeological Unit had appointed a Survey Officer for aerial archaeology and the site was re-located and new photographs taken. It was then seen that the gas pipeline had unwittingly been cut through one of them and half destroyed it. Such unfortunate occurrences are now much less likely to happen as the Unit has built up a comprehensive record of all the sites and monuments so far known in the county, and works closely with planning departments, developers, the Ministry of Transport and other organisations likely to endanger archaeological sites. Much unnecessary destruction is thus avoided.

Ring-ditch is a term used by archaeologists for any circular crop-mark, and some typical ones are on this photograph taken in 1984 at Broome. They, and several other marks, are showing in a field of a ripening cereal crop. Most distinct are two small circles and a large one which touches a double concentric circle, just visible.

Over 900 such ring-ditches have so far been recorded in Norfolk but in very few instances is it possible to state with confidence what was their age or function. For the most part it is certain that the soil thrown up from the cutting of the circular ditches would have formed central mounds or circular banks, but continuous ploughing or intentional levelling has pushed the soil back, so nothing remains on the ground to be seen of what was once a conspicuous feature. Archaeologists consider that the majority are probably the remains of Late Neolithic or Bronze Age burial mounds or 'barrows', especially when they occur in groups. However, only nine ring-ditches have been excavated in Norfolk, of which only one at Bowthorpe was certainly a barrow. One was a windmill stance and the results from the others were inconclusive often because they were badly eroded before excavation began. The larger circle shown here at Broome is an enclosure of some sort with entrances. The double-ditched concentric circle can hardly be anything else but a levelled barrow, similar to those on (10) at Hoveton. Even a goat or horse tied to a pole can create a mark which could be photographed and delude an archaeologist (124), but their general distribution is in agreement with known barrows and a prehistoric date for the majority remains fairly certain.

Warham St Mary hillfort

TF 943 408

Warham is the best preserved of the Iron Age forts in Norfolk, the others being at South Creake, (13) Holkham (14), Narborough, Thetford (15), and a possible one at Tasburgh. Unlike the others, Warham and South Creake are exactly circular. The Warham earthworks enclose an area of 1.4 hectares. There is a pair of banks and ditches which are continuous except for a length now missing in the south-west part of the site where the river Stiffkey was diverted in an eighteenth-century landscaping operation. The original line of the defences beyond the river has been picked up in excavation, and the slight gap in the inner bank, visible on the right-hand side of the photograph, suggests that this might also have been the site of the entrance into the fort. The three other gaps through the defences are all relatively modern. The inner rampart was excavated in 1959 and this revealed foundation trenches for a timber palisade and fighting platform set into the top of the chalk bank. The outer ditch was sectioned and this proved to be 3.3m deep below the old ground surface. The overall height from the present top of the bank to the bottom of the excavated ditch was 9.5m, making the fort with its double line of defences a formidable structure to attack.

Although its shape is very reminiscent of Viking encampments in Denmark the fort is believed to be Iron Age. We have no date for its construction, but several hundred Romano-British pottery sherds excavated from the site are sufficient to show that the defences are pre-Roman and cannot be Danish.

On Bloodgate Hill are the remains of a circular fort badly damaged by deliberate levelling in the early nineteenth century and constant ploughing ever since. Until it was levelled it seems to have been well preserved and similar to Warham (**12**), the main difference being that the South Creake fort had only a single bank and ditch. The outline of the chalk bank and the ditch show up very clearly from the air, but on the ground only a slight earthwork now survives. This is the largest of the Norfolk forts, all presumed to date from the Iron Age. The defences enclosed an area of 3.46 hectares. There are traces of a north-east entrance but otherwise we know very little about the site; it has not been excavated and a geophysical survey in 1973 produced inconclusive results.

Holkham hillfort

TF 874 446

This site is believed to be an Iron Age fort, although its date has not been confirmed by excavation. It sits on the southern tip of a piece of high land which stands proud of the surrounding marshes. This ridge, which can be seen in the picture running northwards into the pine plantation on the sand dunes, is thought to be the tail end of an old sand-spit similar to Scolt Head and Blakeney Point.

The coastline between Holkham and Wells has been much altered in the last two hundred years. The sea originally reached as far as the coast road at Holkham, and there was open water, mud flats and tidal creeks between this coast and the sand-spit. The present belt of pines on the dunes was planted by the second Earl of Leicester in the late nineteenth century to stabilise the sand. The earliest sea bank, about half way across the marsh (not in the picture) was built in 1720, and the final reclamation of all these marshes took place after the building of the Wells sea bank in 1857-9. Now the whole area is valuable grazing land.

The fort was well defended with a bank and ditch along the north side facing the sand-spit. The main entrance was on the south side where there are two defensive banks, and where access was probably only possible by boat. (There is a slight gap in the bank on the north side, which would allow access by land down the sand-spit, but this many not be original.) The site fits well a description by the Roman author Tacitus of a fort which the Roman troops were storming in AD 47-8 to put down a rebellion of the Iceni, but the date and purpose of the site must remain open to speculation for the moment.

Thetford Castle started life as an Iron Age fort and was converted into a motte and bailey castle by the Normans. The Iron Age fort consisted of a double bank and ditch enclosing a bend in the river Thet just where the prehistoric trackway, the Icknield Way, crossed the river. The north and west sides of the fort survive as earthworks, and until 1986 it was thought that Old Market Street and Ford Street (running parallel from left to right at the back of the picture) probably followed the lines of the levelled southern defences. However, ideas had to be revised when excavations by the Norfolk Archaeological Unit in the gardens of Ford Place (the large house to the left of where the two roads meet) showed no sign of ditches where the lines of the two streets continue eastwards to the river. In 1962 excavations by the late Rainbird Clarke across the northern outer bank and ditch revealed two phases of defences both dating to the late Iron Age.

In the eleventh century the very large mound, or 'motte', was built up in the north-west corner of the fort. No doubt, a timber or stone castle keep was then built on top. The inner rampart on the north side was heightened and the whole area then became a Norman castle. The use of the castle seems to have been of short duration and it was apparently demolished, at least in part, late in the twelfth century.*

In May 1980 the Suffolk Archaeological Unit photographed the crop-marks of a large, triple ditched enclosure in a field which was about to be developed as part of the Fison Way industrial estate just north of Thetford (**16**). The site had already attracted interest because of the discovery of a hoard of late Roman silver coins and the Thetford Treasure, a great collection of late Roman silver spoons and gold jewellery.

The latter was found late in 1979 close to the corner of the large white Travenol warehouse, in the top right hand corner of the right-hand photograph. These, and other finds from the Travenol site, all suggested that the enclosure might be a Romano-British temple to which the coins, spoons and jewellery had belonged. Excavations by the Norfolk Archaeological Unit began in August 1980 to investigate the area in advance of the proposed development.

It soon became clear that the site was earlier than had been thought, that it started in the Iron Age, perhaps in the second or first century BC, and that the ditches that showed on the aerial photographs were dug out in the middle of the first century AD when the Iceni, the native people of East Anglia, were special allies of the Roman Empire.

After the topsoil was stripped off by a mechanical excavator, the remains of the ditches, pits and buildings could be seen clearly as dark marks in the pale sand of the hill top. When **17** was taken the western part of the site had been stripped, and the most important remains are visible. Later, the rest of the site out of the top of the photograph was also excavated.

The three ditches showing on the original aerial photograph were not all open at the same time. Originally the two innermost ones were dug in a double square to form an enclosure. Inside were three large circular wooden buildings (seen here in the centre of the photograph looking like oranges cut open) and outside, to the north and the west, were several dozen human burials. Some of these stood inside small circular ditched areas, smaller versions of the earlier Bronze Age ring-ditches (**10 & 11**).

This part of the site was in use in the 40s and 50s AD. Towards the end of the 50s someone, king, chief,

priest, we simply do not know, decided that the site should be elaborated and upgraded. The innermost of the two original ditches was filled in. A new outer ditch was dug, with a wide gap between it and the remaining earlier ditch. This space was filled with long fences, lines of posts set in trenches dug into the ground, and just about visible on the photograph as long straight lines, parallel to the ditches. Inside this new enclosure there was nothing at all, no buildings, no pits, no structures of any sort that were contemporary with it. Perhaps there is a very good reason for this. The new enclosure must have been built in the late 50s AD, perhaps over a few years, with people working on the site for a few weeks each summer. By AD 61, we might imagine that the site was almost finished, and all that remained was to put up the buildings. But that year the great rebellion of Boudicca (Boadicea) broke out, and the men of the tribe swept down to the south burning the cities of Roman Britain. When they were defeated by the Roman army, all work on the site stopped, and the Roman authorities had the ditches filled in and the fences torn down, so that the site could not be used as a stronghold or as a centre of resistance if the rebellion broke out again. It was therefore never finished.

The two phases of enclosures were not necessarily domestic. There is very little rubbish about, and certainly not enough to suggest that the site was ever really lived in. Perhaps it was ceremonial or religious. The great wooden houses, the fences and the ditches would all have been very impressive; we know that there was some sort of Romano-British religious site immediately next door. We will never be sure, but the enclosures on the hill at Thetford may have been a great Icenian religious site, set in the wild sandy waste of Breckland.

This site of a Roman marching camp was first discovered by air photography by the Norfolk Archaeological Unit in 1974. The outline of the camp is defined by the single narrow ditch stretching across three fields with rounded corners all showing up well in this 1974 picture. Later, in 1977 the rest of the fort on the opposite side of the road was identified by further air photography. The whole fort covers 9.8 hectares. Although no finds have yet been recorded from the site, its date is fairly certain from the curved 'playing card' corners typical of Roman military installations. A fort like this may have been occupied for perhaps only a few days or weeks at the most while the army was campaigning and might have been large enough for a legion (nominally 6,000, actually about 4,500 men) on the march.

The small irregular enclosure inside the fort is probably Iron Age, earlier than the fort, and it is unlikely to be related to it.

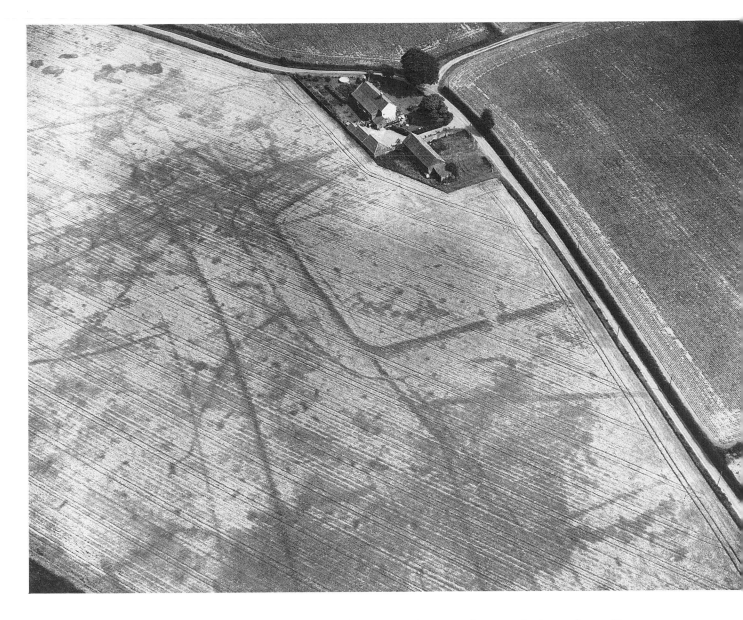

Unlike Horstead with Stanninghall, this cropmark is less easy to interpret because its irregular outline does not conform to the standard pattern for Roman forts. Three sides of the fort are visible with one ditch disappearing under the farmyard at the top of the picture. Nevertheless, the neatly-cut ditch with rounded corners, straight sides and square ends at the entrance suggests a Roman date for the site. Running around inside is a small narrow trench presumably for a timber palisade. Outside the fort is another less regular ditch forming an out work of some description. All over the field is a jumble of other ditches which may or may not be connected to the main site. Across the road, the south side of the fort can just be seen, although further photography will be necessary to pick out all the details.

This is the best preserved Roman monument in Norfolk. It is in the guardianship of the Historic Buildings and Monuments Commission and is open to the public. Until local government re-organisation in 1974 this site was part of Suffolk. The fort overlooks the marshland stretching from Yarmouth to Acle where a salt-water estuary was open to the sea until it was blocked in the Saxon period by the sandspit on which Yarmouth now stands. Burgh Castle, like Brancaster (**21**), was one of a series of 'Saxon Shore' forts built mostly in the third century to defend Britain against increasingly frequent attacks from Anglo-Saxon pirates. The fort, known then as *Gariannonum*, was well situated to provide a base for a part of the Roman fleet to patrol the estuary and the surrounding seas. It has a trapezoidal plan covering *c.* 2 hectares, although the west-facing wall has now gone. Bastions, large circular towers projecting outside the line of the walls, were added during the construction of the walls, unlike Brancaster, which had internal turrets. It was also different from Brancaster in that the walls were built of flint rubble and faced with squared flints interspersed with regular courses of red tiles. The bastions have central holes in their tops, either to carry wall-mounted catapults or, more likely, timber superstructures. The gate can be seen in the middle of the east wall. Air photographs and excavations have so far failed to find any traces of substantial buildings in the interior. Neither have air photographs shown up signs of a civilian settlement outside the fort, as at Brancaster. The site was settled in the Middle Saxon period (seventh-ninth centuries AD). After a period of abandonment the site was used again when it was converted into a castle in the Norman period with a 'motte' or earthen mound to carry a timber keep in the south-west corner.*

Brancaster was one of possibly ten Roman coastal forts built in the third century AD to defend Britain from Anglo-Saxon raiders from across the North Sea. The site is owned by the National Trust and is open to the public, although access is only possible from the coastal footpath which runs along the edge of the salt marshes. Brancaster, or *Branodunum*, was the northernmost of a chain of forts which ran around the coast to Portchester near Portsmouth. Burgh Castle (**20**) near Yarmouth was the next. Unlike Burgh Castle, the walls of the fort at Brancaster do not survive; they were pulled down in 1747.

The fort was roughly square in plan with the great walls built of an imported sandstone, possibly from Kent, enclosing an area of *c.* 2.5 hectares, and it was surrounded by a deep ditch. There were internal square turrets at the corners and gates in the centre of each wall. Little is known about the interior of the fort, although air photography has located some structures including the headquarters building. The purpose of the fort was to provide a base for cavalry units to patrol the coast and also for a part of the Roman fleet to prevent sea-borne raids moving westwards around the coast into the Wash.

At the top of the picture, to the east of the fort, and on a slightly different alignment, is a pattern of rectilinear ditched enclosures and streets indicating the outline of a civilian settlement outside the fort discovered by the Norfolk Archaeological Unit in 1974. The settlement was probably established first, perhaps with an earlier fort, in the second century, and the Shore Fort was laid out later. The earlier fort is assumed to lie under the later one; there might be an even earlier one still, represented by the crop-marks in the bottom left-hand corner of the picture.*

In Roman times the capital of the region was not at Norwich, but at Caistor, 5km to the south. It was known then as Venta Icenorum, the tribal capital of the *Iceni*, the Iron Age tribe which had previously controlled all of Norfolk and north Suffolk. The parish church stands within the ramparts of the Roman town which is owned by the Norfolk Archaeological Trust. The site is now open to the public. This photograph, taken in 1928, shows very clearly the Roman grid-like street pattern, some of the buildings and the rectangular earthen defences. Only one street in the north-east corner does not observe the grid plan, which was laid out in the first century AD. The town defences were built later, in the third century, enclosing an area of 14 hectares, and excluding some streets visible at the bottom of the photograph. Either the town had not filled the whole area as originally laid out or the population had shrunk in size over the two centuries.

Excavations in the 1930s revealed the 'forum' - the town hall - public baths and temples, some of which can just be seen in the picture.

In the fields around the Roman town an Anglo-Saxon cemetery and evidence of settlement have been found, raising an interesting question of how long the Caistor area remained an important centre after the Roman period and why Norwich started to develop as the new regional centre some five centuries later. The transfer from Caistor to Norwich sometime during the seventh to ninth centuries is a subject which will certainly repay more detailed research.*

**Brampton
Roman town**

TG 223 237

Unlike Caistor St Edmund (**22**), Brampton was not recognised as a substantial Roman settlement until intensive fieldwork began in the area in 1966. Roman urns were found at Brampton in 1667, but the precise location of that discovery was not recorded. Since the 1960s fieldwork and air photography have revealed a Roman town with defences forming an irregular 6-hectare hexagon. The defensive ditches forming four sides of this hexagon can be seen in the picture. It is just possible to see a gap in the ditch on the west (left) side where the main east-to-west Roman road, which crosses Norfolk from Denver to the east coast (**26**) enters the town. Alongside this road as it approached the town there was a substantial industrial suburb where at least 140 pottery kilns have been recorded from scatters of pottery and burning in the ploughsoil.

Brampton can now be seen as a small defended town serving as a market centre with a prosperous pottery industry. But, as with so many Roman sites in the region, it did not survive the end of Roman rule; indeed, there are in Norfolk and Suffolk no Roman towns or trading centres of significance which persisted into the Middle Ages.

The railway was built on an embankment across the Roman town in 1874 as part of the line from Wroxham to Reepham.

24

Peddars Way
Roman road

TF 737 334

The Peddars Way is a Roman road which comes up from Suffolk and then runs across Norfolk from Brettenham in the south to Holme-next-the-Sea on the north-west coast. It is particularly straight with only one bend, at Hockham. Few Roman roads in the region are quite so straight. It must have been built as a long distance route, although its destination is not clear. At Holme there is no significant settlement to justify the enormous effort involved in its construction. One theory is that Holme was just an embarkation point for a ferry across the Wash to join up with a similar Roman road which came down to the sea near Skegness.

Seen from the air here on the chalk upland at Fring, and on the map, the road is an impressive feature in the landscape. However, because it is not followed today by any significant routes, much of it is made up of farm tracks and country lanes ideal for the rambler. The road is now the route for a long-distance walk sponsored by the Countryside Commission and Norfolk County Council. A booklet on the walk is available from the Commission.

Also conspicuous in this photograph are the large rectangular fields laid out mainly in the eighteenth and nineteenth centuries, and their pits which were dug to produce clay subsoil or 'marl' for spreading on the light land.*

One of the significant innovations of the seventeenth-century drainage of the fens was the construction of two parallel channels, the Bedford Rivers (**118-9**), about half a mile apart. Between the two rivers is an area known as the Washes; in the winter this acts as a gigantic reservoir for floodwater while in the summer it provides pasture; the area shown in the picture is a nature reserve flooded deliberately for breeding birds. Apart from the Old Bedford River running diagonally across the top of the photo, the two most obvious features are the sinuous light-coloured bands showing against the darker floodwater. These ridges mark the course of natural watercourses which drained the fens of the Welney area before the Roman period. Known as roddons, they result from the formation of levees – banks of flood silt beside the river – which gradually merged leaving only a narrow central channel for the water flow. Such a central channel can be clearly see on the more distant roddon. Because of their extra height roddons provided convenient locations for settlement and communication links, both in the distant and in the more recent past. In the photograph the roddon in the left foreground supports the A1101, the main road from Littleport to Wisbech. On the other roddon, adjacent to the central channel, can be seen several rectangular enclosures defined by the dark lines of ditches and, closer to the foreground, the parallel ditches of a contemporary trackway. All these represent parts of a Roman settlement occupied first in the second century AD and then again in the third to fourth centuries.

Downham West Fen Causeway and Roman Field System

TF 571 004

On the siltlands around the Wash and along the edge of the peat fens traces of Roman settlement and industrial activity are plentiful. However, prior to their drainage in the seventeenth century, the peat fens provided a considerable obstacle to travel. Of the few Roman roads which traversed this boggy region the Fen Causeway was undoubtedly the most significant. It started near Castor just to the west of Peterborough and running via the island of March it reached the Norfolk upland at Denver near Downham Market; there the road split, one line, probably the more important but not yet very well known, running across Norfolk, through Watton to Caistor St Edmund, and a second road running further north to Smallburgh in east Norfolk, and possibly on to Caister-on-Sea. For much of its course in the Norfolk fens the Fen Causeway, which can still be detected as a plough-disturbed layer of gravel, follows the southern side of a roddon (**25**). Its sinuous course is clearly discernible as a light mark in the Washes between the Bedford Rivers and can be traced westwards into the foreground of the photograph. A little further to the west the roddon is so straight that it must have originated as a deliberately constructed Roman canal. At one point within the photographed area the remains of a Roman bridge which crossed a tributary stream were excavated in 1933. But, the clearest demonstration of Roman activity is the large number of rectangular blocks of land defined by ditches on the northern side of the roddon. These represent the paddocks and fields of a highly organised settlement adjacent to the road, which was certainly in use in the third century A D. Curious features such as the multitude of small square enclosures just to the north-east of the farm buildings and the groups of dark pit-like marks to the east remain to be explained.

**Spong Hill,
North Elmham**

TF 982 195

Since the early eighteenth century, pots containing cremated bones and grave-goods have been dug up on the top of Spong Hill, a site which overlooks the Blackwater Valley. Modern agricultural damage to this Early Saxon cemetery prompted a long-term rescue excavation by the Norfolk Archaeological Unit from 1972 to 1981. The photograph shows these excavations taking place in the summer of 1977. They revealed Neolithic pits with pottery and flints, Roman ditches containing domestic rubbish, Early Saxon cremations in pots, and several graves. Some of these Early Saxon graves were inside ring-ditches, and were probably originally covered by a mound.

Many seasons of excavation have added to the history of Spong Hill - a site occupied intermittently in the early prehistoric period, and more permanently from the Late Iron Age, with extensive remains of a Roman farmstead and its field system. The Anglo-Saxons used the site as a cemetery, burying over 2,000 cremations mostly in urns, and laying out fifty-seven of their dead in graves. This cemetery occupied the edge of the hilltop in the fifth and sixth centuries AD. To the north, west, and east, the post-holes and impressions of at least nine wooden buildings have been excavated. This suggests that an unexcavated settlement contemporary with the cemetery still lies below the ploughsoil on the rest of Spong Hill.

The crop-marks seen in the photograph are evidence of post-medieval field boundaries (which can be seen on nineteenth-century maps), Roman fields, a late Iron Age boundary, and probable Bronze Age burial mounds (one ploughed-out example shows clearly as a ring-ditch in the centre of the photograph).

Bichamditch, Beachamwell

TG 745 084

This photograph shows one of the few earthworks which survive from the early part of the Anglo-Saxon period; they date from the two centuries after the end of Roman rule, but who actually built them and why is still the subject of much speculation. The bank and ditch of this earthwork called the Bichamditch can be seen here crossing the line of the Roman road just to the east of Marham airfield (off the picture to the right). The Roman road follows the main road in the left-hand part of the picture up to the dyke; on the right-hand side the road swings away to the south, but the line of the Roman road can just be seen continuing straight on as a field boundary.

The dyke, running 7 km north to south from Narborough to Caldecote with its ditch facing east, was built at a time when Roman rule had collapsed and the region was divided by apparently hostile groups. Anglo-Saxon invading settlers were imposing a new culture on the sub-Roman communities; friction between the various groups was inevitable. The dyke runs at right angles to the Roman road, and for about 1 km to either side of the road it was more substantially constructed than for the rest of its route.

The dyke was, therefore, intended to control movement along the road from the east and was constructed after the Roman period and before the Anglo-Saxons had established a united kingdom over the whole of East Anglia in the seventh century. To the south is another similar earthwork called the Fossditch, seen best at Cranwich, running between the Wissey and Little Ouse. This also faces east and it was perhaps part of the same defensive system separating part of West Norfolk and the fens from the rest of the county.

The earthworks of the motte and bailey castle at Horsford, known as Castle Yards or Castle Hill, are under pasture and protected as an Ancient Monument. The motte is now not much taller than the banks of the bailey. The overall plan, a circular ditched motte impinging on a circular bailey, is an early form of castle, the best example of which in the east of England may be seen at Pleshey in Essex. There are suggestions on the photograph of foundations of a stone keep on top of the motte, and of a gateway or barbican between the motte and bailey.

The castle was founded in the late eleventh-century by Walter de Cadomo; the stone keep, if such it was, would probably have been added in the twelfth century. By 1431 it was in a state of decay. A large deer park to the north is still remembered by the name Black Park.

Castle Acre castle

TF 818 151

After the Norman Conquest, William I gave *Acra* to William de Warenne, who later became Earl of Surrey. His castle controlled the Peddars Way (**24**) and the ford over the Nar. In the twelfth century the town with its rectangular layout to the west was defended by a ditch and bank (visible in the top right-hand corner of the picture), crowned with a palisade or wall, and with two gateways.

The castle, seen here under excavation in 1976, consists of an upper ward (to the north), a lower ward (to the south), and a defended outwork, the barbican (to the east). The building in the upper ward contained the lord's hall and private apartments, as well as an undercroft for storage. The lower ward would have contained stabling, workshops, storehouses and retainers' living quarters.

Excavations in the upper ward revealed a complex building sequence. By 1085 an impressive country house stood within a courtyard surrounded by a palisaded bank and ditch. Within a few years, the original wooden gateway, giving access to the lower ward, was replaced in stone. Around 1140 the house was converted into a keep, and the defences were strengthened. Although the scale of the keep was reduced, the finished result would have been very impressive. However, in the later twelfth century the upper ward was abandoned.

In the lower ward, parch marks in the grass reveal the foundations of buildings. It is suggested that these are of thirteenth-century date – a hall with private chambers, pantry (for storage of food), and a buttery (for storage of butts of wine and ale), a detached kitchen, and possibly a chapel. The lower ward had a substantial gatehouse facing the town, and a smaller one facing the barbican.

Documentary evidence suggests that the castle declined in importance during the fourteenth century, and finally went out of use. In later years it was used as a source of building stone for the houses nearby.*

The massive earthworks of the castle dominate their surroundings. It is not difficult to see why Victorian antiquaries believed the central enclosure had cut in two a Roman fort, but excavations in 1970-76 proved that the whole assemblage (including the much fainter western bailey, to the left) is Norman. The stone keep, with elaborate arcading similar to Norwich castle (**95**), was erected by the d'Albini family in 1138, as was the gatehouse; a curtain wall around the inner bailey was built in the fourteenth century and demolished in the eighteenth. The foundations visible on the near side of the keep belong to buildings in part added when Queen Isabella was imprisoned here after her part in the murder of her husband, Edward II. The remains within the rectangle just beyond the keep are those of the original Saxo-Norman parish church, secularised when the castle was built around it. It was replaced by the present Norman church towards the top of the photograph (the belfry is Victorian).

The generally rectilinear layout of the village may suggest that this is a Norman planned town, as at Castle Acre (**30**) and New Buckenham (**32**), but detailed evidence is lacking. The town decayed in the later Middle Ages, as told in the old Norfolk rhyme 'Rising was a seaport, when Lynn it was a Marsh. Now Lynn it is a seaport, and Rising fares the warse'; most of the houses visible are less than two hundred years old. However, to the right of the church may be seen the courtyard of the Trinity Hospital, almshouses constructed between 1600 and 1614.*

New Buckenham town and castle

TM 088 905

New Buckenham is a rare example of a Norman planned town that has not significantly expanded outside or shrunk within its original boundaries. This view shows the castle in the foreground, the town layout beyond, and at the top the common. William d'Albini carved the parish of New Buckenham out of that of Old Buckenham in 1146, abandoning his castle there which he handed over to Augustinian monks to prevent it being held against him. Interestingly the new castle is still in Old Buckenham parish; only the town and common comprise New Buckenham.

Standing within the main ringwork are the remains of the earliest shell keep in Britain (1145-50). Behind it can be seen the east bailey, and the original entrance was in a direct line with the central street of the town. In the thirteenth century the south west bailey was added; its cropmarks are visible in the extreme foreground. The building on the right-hand side of the square of farm buildings to the right of the keep is the original castle chapel.

It is not clear whether the group of houses just behind this chapel is part of the original layout; otherwise, the town is contained within a defensive ditch, only the farms at top right having crossed this. The grid pattern of streets, as at Castle Acre (**30**) and Castle Rising (**31**), still largely remains; the market place (top centre, crossed by a later diagonal road) once extended another block to the right. Evidence suggests that the town was not at first totally built up; the modern houses at the bottom left corner of the town stand on plots that were abandoned and given back to Old Buckenham parish. Among the present houses in the town are fine late medieval structures. The church was founded around 1240 but was much rebuilt 1479-1509 and in 1870.*

Binham priory lies to the north of the village, in its own precinct, with a gatehouse to the west. There were fishponds to the north east next to the river Stiffkey, where there was a watermill.

The priory was founded in the late eleventh century by Peter de Valoines and his wife Albreda, as a dependant house of the Benedictine Abbey of St. Albans. The building works were not completed until the mid-thirteenth century, and changes and additions went on into the fifteenth century. In 1539 the priory was dissolved by Henry VIII and sold to Thomas Paston. His grandson Edward pulled down some of the buildings to re-use the stone, but the nave of the church was kept for use by the parish.

The central part of the plan was the cloister walk, with a lean-to roof providing sheltered access to the buildings on all four sides. On the north side was the church, dominated by a tower over the crossing. North and south of the ruined piers of the crossing tower were the transepts, to the east the monks choir and side chapels, and to the west the nave. Inside the nave is an interesting progression in architectural styles, from the Norman at the east end, to the Early English at the west end, culminating in a beautiful west window, bricked up in the early nineteenth century (not visible in the picture).

The range west of the cloisters contained the outer parlour, for transactions with the outside world, the cellarer's range for storage of provisions, and probably accommodation for the Prior and guests. The south range contained the refectory, served by a kitchen to the south.

The east range consisted of the chapter house, monks' parlour and warming room, and an undercroft. The monks' dormitory was on the first floor, with access to the reredorter (toilets). A malting kiln, which was probably used into the eighteenth century, occupied its own building at the south end of the range. It was part of a complex of buildings with brewing and baking facilities for supplying the priory.*

West Dereham abbey

TF 662 006

The crop-marks of West Dereham abbey buildings do not normally show up from the air at all, but the photographer caught this extraordinarily detailed record of the site during the drought of 1976. The site is on the fen edge and in most years the water table is not low enough to provide stress conditions in the crops to make marks appear, but 1976 was exceptional. The site is on private land; but a public right of way follows the track that winds across the photograph, and another footpath joins it from the top left.

The abbey was founded in 1188 as a 'Premonstratensian' monastery and dissolved in 1539. In 1695 or thereabouts, Sir Thomas Derham, returning from office as ambassador to Tuscany and Genoa, constructed a large mansion, in the Tuscan style of a century earlier, centred on the still standing gatehouse of the Abbot's Lodging. Some tiny ruins of this remain in the clump of trees in the centre. At bottom left is a ruined coach house which incorporates a buttress and a lancet window, probably the only standing remains of the abbey itself. Sir Thomas planted the screen of trees around the site.

The monastic church in the middle of the picture is difficult to pick out because it is obscured by so much rubble in the soil. Around this, though, there is much in evidence. The buttressed outer gatehouse can be seen at the back of the picture and from there a road showing as a light-coloured strip runs down the picture to where the west end of the church stood. To the right of the gatehouse is a large barn. Various buildings, including the chapter house, can be seen around the cloisters and to the right of these is a separate group of buildings identified as the 'infirmary' or hospital. Near the bottom of the picture is a substantial rectangular building possibly the 'reredorter' or latrine block. All this shows how much can be revealed about a site without putting a spade into the ground at all.

Wymondham abbey

TG 106 015

In 1107 the d'Albini family gave their manor house (believed to have stood at the extreme left centre of the photograph) as a site for a new Benedictine priory. The foundation grew over the centuries and in 1449 it was upgraded to an abbey.

The church was shared by monks and townspeople; disagreements between them reached such a pitch that an appeal was made to Pope Innocent IV in 1249 which resulted in the town gaining the nave, north aisle and former north-west tower, and the monks the south aisle, south-west tower, and the remainder. This complicated arrangement was never really satisfactory and around 1400 the monks built a wall between nave and choir, with a tower above, to appropriate the east end and abandon their part in the nave. In reply the townspeople determined to build a new west tower higher than the monks', and this was eventually done in 1461-73. Sixty years later the abbey was dissolved and the monastic sections of the church demolished, leaving only the shell of the central tower and a few scattered fragments of walls as a monument to the monks' pride.

The photograph shows the church with the west tower further from the camera, and the monks' tower with the foundations of the choir in front of it. The marks of the cloisters and ancillary buildings to the left were only revealed by aerial photography in 1979 and have not yet been surveyed in detail.*

The windswept and desolate island of Cowholme gives little indication today of its former grandeur as one of the most powerful monasteries in the region. Founded in AD 800 (and legends speak of an even earlier house) the present remains are those of a Benedictine abbey endowed in 1020.

Pilgrims approached the island along the causeway from Horning (top left). The structure resembling a factory chimney is the brick cone of an eighteenth-century windmill covering the fourteenth-century gatehouse. The mill ground cole seed and rape seed to produce 'Colza oil' for lamps and pumped water. The eighteenth-century antiquary Sir John Fenn raged at this 'vandalism' yet ironically the mill has preserved the carvings on the gateway. To the right of this the monastic fishponds may be seen. Running across the picture behind the fishponds is the line of the perimeter wall. In the centre of the photograph are the foundations of the church, and along the river bank are various buildings whose walls, eroded out by the current, have claimed the keels of many holiday cruisers.

After the Dissolution, when monastries were abolished, the materials of the church were shipped to Norwich for use in building the Duke of Norfolk's Palace, whilst the Bishop of Norwich (whose titles include Abbot of St Benet's) appropriated the carved woodwork. Some buildings remained, one becoming the Chequers Inn, a favourite haunt of wherrymen until it was burnt down in the nineteenth century.*

Less famous than the Augustinian priory in Walsingham, the Franciscan friary is nevertheless of great interest. Founded in 1346, the main road was diverted to its present position (top of photograph) in 1351 as construction progressed.

The tallest surviving remains are those of the guesthouse (left foreground) constructed in blissful ignorance of the future not long before the friary was dissolved in 1538. Behind the early Victorian house, attached, can be seen the gable of the frater (dining hall) with the kitchens to the right. Behind the kitchen is the Little Cloister, a remarkable fifteenth-century structure whose walkways were totally enclosed, as the surviving slab of wall with its windows shows. Behind the guesthouse, the garden plots aligned left to right and the long plot with a central tree mark the site of the Great Cloister. The Chapter House is in the clump of bushes beyond. The friary church stood to the left of these ruins and has long since gone. The church belfry contained the Great Bell of Walsingham, given to the parish church when the church was pulled down.

The ruins are occasionally open to the public in summer.

Moats at West Carr, Attleborough

TM 023 947

Over 400 medieval moated sites dot the Norfolk landscape, especially in the boulder clay region of the centre and south of the county. Their present conditions vary: some still surround late medieval or later houses (74), some survive as earthworks in woods and meadows, while others have been ploughed flat and can only be seen as crop marks (39). Many moats enclosed manor houses and others contained farms both usually built of wood and clay. Manors and farms would have been surrounded by subsidiary agricultural buildings often placed within moated, ditched or walled outer enclosures. Almost all were constructed between the later twelfth and fourteenth centuries.

Although defence against minor attacks might have been a reason for moat digging, as was the necessity for drainage on the heavier soils, the main impetus was status and fashion, with the landed gentry and wealthier farmers emulating the mighty defensive castles of the baronial class.

This fine example at West Carr, Attleborough, may have been the site of Little Rectory or Westker manor. It lies on either side of a stream (a headwater of the Thet) in meadowland. Somewhat unusually it was not marked on Ordnance Survey maps, and was discovered from the air in 1984.

This fine trapezoidal moated enclosure at Grimston was not recorded as an archaeological site by the Ordnance Survey, although it survived intact as a grassland earthwork to be photographed by the RAF in 1946. At sometime since then, however, it has been levelled and ploughed, and here we see the remarkably clear outlines of the main features visible as cropmarks in 1976. Although more obvious from the air than the Attleborough example (**38**), this site has been largely destroyed, with most of the delicate archaeological evidence for buildings, yard surfaces and floors long since removed by ploughing. To the left of the moat can be seen a pair of rectangular fishponds supplied with water, like the moat itself, by a spring at centre top. Other filled-in ditches can be seen in the top left, while in the foreground what appears to be three sides of a ditched enclosure was in fact a pond in 1946. The moat lies on glacial gravels in the spring-line below the chalk escarpment, and the water drained away to bottom left to become the Gaywood River.

It has not been possible to identify which, if any, of the nine medieval manors of Grimston was situated here. As there is only one other moated site known in the parish perhaps the remaining manor houses were not moated.

In the meadow beside Pudding Norton Hall are the earthworks of a fine example of a deserted village, together with the ruins of the parish church standing close to the west side of the field. This site, together with another one nearby at Godwick (**41**), represents a class of site which has almost disappeared as a result of the ploughing up of old meadowland in recent years. Like Godwick, the village of *Nortuna*, as it was originally called, decayed gradually with the population decline of the fifteenth and sixteenth centuries. Rural population seems to have reached its peak in the fourteenth century and then dropped dramatically as a result of plagues, bad harvests and poor weather thereafter.

The farm track running north to south through the meadow is the line of the village street, and the banks and ditches running away at right angles from it are the toft or property divisions within the village. On the east side of the street there are thirteen tofts and on the west nine. Little trace of the houses remains above ground because they were made either of timber or clay. The only medieval building to survive is the church which has a tower of Saxo-Norman date. A close examination of the pattern of the village earthworks here suggests that there was an element of planning in the layout of the village. Several boundary banks on one side of the street are directly opposite similar ones on the opposite side. There is also a certain uniformity of width, and several of the longer tofts have rear banks at equal distance from the street. While the planning of towns is to be expected (**30-32**), it is perhaps surprising to find it in villages as well.

Like Pudding Norton (**40**), Godwick is also a deserted medieval village. Unlike Pudding Norton, however, the medieval earthworks are not so extensive because the village site was reorganised in the seventeenth century as part of a landscaping scheme for Godwick Hall. The site is therefore of interest because it represents two distinct periods of activity quite different in nature – one, the medieval village, the other, the gardens, orchards and paddocks for the hall. The hall was built in 1558, but the area around was not laid out as we see it from the earthworks until the seventeenth century. The site is open to the public during the summer and can be approached from Godwick Hall Farm. The Historic Buildings and Monuments Commission has recently erected interpretation panels with air photographs and plans on the site.

Running down the site is the sunken line of the village street with two roads leading off to the right. In the angle of one of these is the church. Running away from the main street on both sides are ditches forming the divisions between the properties or 'tofts' of the medieval village.

Further back is the long seventeenth-century barn built over the line of the street. To the right of that are the earthworks of rectilinear enclosures around the site of the hall. The hall itself is only just visible as a square in the middle of these since its ruins were pulled down in 1961. The church tower, standing proud within the village earthworks, is largely a seventeenth-century folly. It was built on the foundations of the original tower partly in brick and partly out of the stonework of the old church pulled down at the time.*

**Hockwold
shrunken village,
Hockwold
cum Wilton**

TL 727 878

While some villages were deserted altogether in the Middle Ages and later (**40, 41 & 43**), many more just shrank in size, often creating gaps around greens or along village streets. Hockwold is an example where a whole area of a village seems to have been abandoned, leaving remarkable earthworks. The sunken line of a street can be seen running diagonally across the picture. There are also numerous boundary banks and ditches, pits and hollows, many of which are difficult to interpret.

Hockwold is on the edge of the fens and was an area heavily settled in prehistoric and Roman times. The slighter earthworks in the foreground are the remains of a Roman settlement which previously spread out well to the east and west of the area shown in the photograph, but unfortunately much of this evidence has since been lost due to ploughing. In addition, since this photograph was taken in 1962 the fenland 'Cut Off Channel' has been dug right through the area shown in the picture.

Running north to south across the Roman earthworks are earthworks and hedgerows of long narrow strip fields, presumably medieval in origin since they butt against the disused street described above. This is a fine example of a site with earthworks of different dates overlying and adjoining each other.

Greynston
deserted village,
Tittleshall

TF 907 198

Greynston (called 'Grenstein' on Ordnance Survey maps) was a medieval village which began as a settlement on the heavy clay upland soils of central Norfolk in the eleventh or twelfth century at a time when the rural population was expanding and cultivation was moving into more marginal areas. The site was deserted in the fifteenth century during population decline. Unlike the other deserted and shrunken villages described (40-42), this site is now entirely ploughed.

Greynston had a manor house, a village, two greens, two commons, fields and woods, with its manorial bounds extending from Tittleshall to Mileham. The main settlement area survived as an earthwork site until 1959. This photograph was taken soon after the humps and bumps were bulldozed and then ploughed. It is a sad example of how so many earthwork sites have been destroyed in this way in the last thirty or forty years. The soil-marks showing fresh after the first ploughing reveal the plan of the village very well.

The picture shows the line of the village street running diagonally down the field with the rectangular 'tofts' or properties along the right hand side. To the left was a village pond at the head of a triangular green. Traces of further tofts can be seen along the left-hand side of the green.

One toft was excavated in 1963-4 to reveal a clay-built (probably 'clay lump') farmhouse with flint cobbled yards and outbuildings around. Many of the light soil-marks showing up within the tofts down the right-hand side of the street are also other similar clay-built houses or outbuildings.

'The common pasture of Fritton Called Fritton Green' - thus was the magnificent stretch of ancient common described in 1827. This area of the country, on heavy boulder clay, is blessed with an above average survival of medieval commons. These heaths and commons, on badly drained clay upland, poor sandy soils and in river valleys - the pieces less suitable for arable farming - were of great importance to the rural economy of the Middle Ages. They provided, for those with commoning rights, areas of pasture at times when other grazing was not available. They were also sources of clay for house building and for marling the fields, as the pits in the centre of the picture show.

The edges of the commons were frequently settled by peasants, from the eleventh or twelfth centuries onwards, although as areas of common grazing they are almost certainly older, probably Anglo-Saxon.

The importance of common land led to its slow removal; it was nibbled away first by encroachment and then by enclosure so that whereas today less than 1% of Norfolk's land area is common, at the beginning of the nineteenth century it was as high as 11%.

Fieldwalking suggests that the original settlement was around the parish church of Fritton (background) which has a Saxo-Norman tower. Colonisation of the area around the green seems to have begun at a relatively early date - Fritton Hall (in trees right of the crossroads at the far end of the green) is a mid-sixteenth century building, but eleventh-century pottery has been found in its garden and it may be on the site of a manor house. Frittonend Farm (foreground) and the cottages on the opposite side of the green, show how the settlement slowly spread southwards.*

Many Norfolk villages have a green, but few are as large as Church Green at Old Buckenham. It takes its name from the parish church (top centre of photograph) which has stood here since Norman times, having been extended in the fourteenth century. Some houses along the same side of the green date to the sixteenth century, but the other sides have buildings of more recent date – those in the front of the photograph are all twentieth century – and it is not known how far the original village spread around the green.

The two ponds – one between the church and the road bisecting the green surrounded by trees, the other beside the road forming the left-hand boundary of the green – may be old clay or gravel pits, illustrating the ancient right to dig for such materials from common land. Several of the plots fronting the green were at one time used to grow hemp for ropemaking.

The clump of trees beyond the school rugby posts (top left corner) marks a mysterious hillock, believed by some to be a burial mound and by others to be a later landscaping feature.*

The common of Alderford, some 14 hectares in extent, straddles the Norwich to Reepham road some 14 km from the city. It lies in the south-west corner of the parish of Swannington and is a plateau of sandy glacial loam sloping down to the north west into a valley of a small south-flowing tributary of the river Wensum. Much of the south-eastern quarter has been quarried for the chalk which underlies the site, having been deposited from further north during the Ice Age.

This chalky rubble in the pit bottom supports an interesting collection of chalk-loving wild plants, although the photograph really shows how overgrown with Hawthorn and Blackthorn scrub the area has become since the traditional grazing of the common, carried on since the Middle Ages with cattle, goats and chickens, petered out during the 1960s.

An overgrown Bronze Age round barrow on the left-hand side of the picture belongs to an earlier time, and its survival indicates that this land may never have been ploughed.

The survival of this common, which is one of the Nature Conservancy Councils Sites of Special Scientific Interest, is indeed fortunate since so many other areas have been ploughed up or afforested.

The great curve of hedgerows visible in the centre of the photograph marks the eastern and southern boundaries of the hunting park attached to the d'Albini's Wymondham manor house, still fossilized in the landscape after nine hundred years. The line starts at the top left-hand corner; at the far right, where the hedgerow ends at a clump of trees, a soil-mark can be seen continuing the line which extends for another half mile or so beyond the photograph's edge. The hedgerow in the distance, apparently forming the far side of the park, may not in fact be its boundary at all - it marks the line of the Bays River and the park may have extended further west.

Lower Park Farm, in the centre of the photograph, was formerly Grishaugh or Greatpark Farm, and occupies the site of the Norman hunting lodge whose moat remains. In the wood beyond are traces of what may be a second moated site. On the extreme right-hand centre of the photograph is the edge of Park Farm, formerly Cromwell or Littlepark Farm. The names of the two farms illustrate how the park was divided between the manors of Grishaugh and Cromwell's in the Wymondham 'Outsoken' into the Great and Little parks.

The d'Albinis clearly enjoyed the chase, as Silfield and the even greater park at Old Buckenham show.

There were once four churches in Shotesham; All Saints in High Shotesham (**49**) and St Botolph, St Mary and St Martin in Low Shotesham. St Mary's (centre right of photograph) contains work of around 1200, and was extended around 1300 and in 1468. The tower was being built in 1534 but in 1602 the church was roofless; it was restored in 1879. St Martin's (foreground) is said to have had Saxon work visible (it was mentioned in the reign of Edward the Confessor); the remaining tower is of the early fourteenth century and serves as a home for owls and kestrels. St Botolph's has entirely vanished; its site is beyond the top of the picture.

Low Shotesham seems to have declined early, for though finds made in recent years indicate Late Saxon and twelfth-century occupation, yet St Botolph's and St Mary's parishes were merged as early as 1311. The Nomina Villarum of 1316 (a list of villages able to raise men at arms for the Bishop of Norwich) includes the village under High Shotesham. In 1428 there were only ten householders, and in 1516 the Enclosure Commissioners found that 'St Mary's parish has been enclosed to the detriment of the commoners'. Towards the top of the photograph a few earthworks of the roads and house plots may be seen.

The ring of trees (upper left) mark the moated site around the Old Hall, though the present building is only a remnant of a mansion dating from around 1700; but it may have an older core.*

All Saints Church, for long the last of the Shotesham churches to remain in use (**48**) stands proudly on an abrupt natural mound above the river valley. From this hill the village derives its old name, sadly nowadays abandoned in favour of the more prosaic Shotesham All Saints. Most of the village fabric of the church dates from the early fourteenth century, but a drastic restoration in 1899 added several features – including a stone vulture on the gable, looking eastward for the Second Coming with the keenest sight of all birds.

To the left of the church is the old school, attached to an Elizabethan thatched house reputedly once the rectory; the park of the Regency rectory extends behind it. Across the road from this stands Tollgate Cottage, an interesting fifteenth-century building. In the foreground centre at the road junction is the former Dukes Head Inn, rebuilt in 1712 by the Mingay family with beams from an older building. The common across the road has happily escaped encroachment by modern housing and is now designated as a Site of Special Scientific Interest by the Nature Conservancy Council.*

The ruins in North Elmham village showing in this picture are open to the public; indeed, the site is well worth a visit and it provides some fine views across the Wensum valley. Signs to the site will tell the visitor he is approaching an Anglo-Saxon cathedral, but scholars now hotly dispute whether the stonework is Anglo-Saxon or indeed whether it ever was a cathedral.

The site is known locally as Tower Hills. It is quite clear that the ruins do represent an early church, with a massive square western tower, a long narrow nave, transepts and a small semi-circular apse at the east end. However, the ruins are confusing for the visitor because in the fourteenth century the church was converted into a manor house by Bishop Despenser of Norwich when he defended the manor by piling up banks of earth around the building. The whole site is also surrounded by a massive outer ditch clearly visible in the photograph.

There is no argument that the site is actually the same as the one on which the Saxon cathedral stood, for the remains of an enormous burial ground have been found around it stretching as far south as the parish church. The discussion surrounds the date of the much-altered ruins. Some have argued that the church could date to before the Norman Conquest and actually be the cathedral built before the bishops moved away in 1071; while others are sure that there is nothing at all which need be Anglo-Saxon and the whole structure could be Norman, possibly a chapel for the manor house retained by the bishops who continued to own the property after the move. Evidence at the moment favours the latter view.*

St George's Church at Shimpling stands isolated among fields to the south of its tiny village, but it is approached by public rights of way from three directions suggesting that there was once habitation around it. The north door, facing the Hall, has always been the main entrance, and, as can be seen, the north side of the churchyard has more gravestones than the south. The old story of the 'Devil's Acre' on the north side clearly had few believers here.

There are traces of Saxon or Norman work in the nave, and the round tower has a set of circular belfry windows at its top, now blocked up and rediscovered in 1987. The polygonal belfry stage was added above these probably in the fourteenth century, with four bell openings and imitation flint-and-flush-work tracery on the other faces. The weight of the new top stage seems to have cracked the tower, which is stitched in Late Medieval brickwork. The spire dates from 1874. The chancel is late thirteenth century, with a roof reconstructed in 1633; the nave was given new windows, doors and roof in the fifteenth century. A thorough restoration was undertaken by the architect E.G. Lee in 1867-74.*

St Peter and St Paul, Sall (or Salle; pronounced Saul) represents many people's idea of the typical isolated Norfolk church. The photograph cannot reflect adequately its great yellow bulk, or the way in which for miles around just the pinnacled tower appears above the low hills, like a great brooding long-eared-owl.

The building is one of those rare structures which can be firmly dated in a number of ways. Apart from two windows, which are probably Victorian, it is all of the fifteenth century. The west doorway bears the arms of Henry V (1405 -20), a south window formerly had a date 1411, the north transept was recorded in 1440 and the south in 1444. The church, therefore, was erected between 1405 and 1445, although the heraldry on the south transept's parapet indicates a reconstruction of its south wall later in the century. The interior contains many delights including original painted woodwork.

The three other buildings in the photograph were (left to right) the school, smithy and public house. There are no other buildings in the immediate vicinity and there is not enough evidence to judge whether a village ever surrounded the church, or whether it has always stood alone in an area of scattered farmsteads.*

There are more ruined rural medieval parish churches in Norfolk than in the rest of England combined. A high population and great wealth in the Middle Ages led to the building of many churches. Rural population decline, the movement of settlement, a reduction of the importance of the Established Church in the minds of many people, coupled with the increase in the relative cost of repairs, have caused the abandonment of almost two hundred churches since the fifteenth century. Some are romantic ruins today, others no more than a scatter of mortared flint and broken human bones in an arable field. The sites of a few have been lost completely. Tivetshall St Mary, most of which dates from *c.* 1300, is untypical in that it was a thriving church until 1947 when a passing plane brought down the west tower over the nave. The church was never rebuilt, although the graveyard is still in use; the sister church of Tivetshall St Margaret now serves the two parishes. The medieval village that worshipped at St Mary's lay not around the church but around a large green to the east. There was a church here in the eleventh century and it is possible that in Late Saxon times settlement was closer to the church. No fieldwork has yet been carried out to test this possibility.*

Crop-marks of church, Itteringham

TG 154 303 ◄●

The site of this lost church at Itteringham was only discovered in 1986 while the Archaeological Unit's survey officer was on a routine air photography flight over the area. The crop-marks in this picture show three buildings, including a church with a nave 6 m wide and a slightly narrower apse to the east. This simple plan is typical of churches of Late Saxon or Norman date built in the eleventh or twelfth centuries. Just to the south of that is a fragment of a building which does not otherwise show up as a cropmark. To the south of that again is a large rectangular building, 18 m long, possibly a manor house or some other substantial domestic structure.

This group of buildings can probably be identified as Nowers Manor; the church is most likely the chapel of St Nicholas mentioned in 1310 and 1430. It may have been a parish church at one time, but by the fifteenth century it was a chapel, possibly a private chapel for the manor. The plan shows that it was not enlarged or altered significantly during its lifetime, unlike the site at Ormesby St Margaret (**55**).

The large building to the south is probably the manorial hall, but whether it is as early as the church is a matter which could only be established by careful excavation.

The Rev. Francis Blomefield, author of the famous History of Norfolk, recorded in the early eighteenth century a journey on which he passed, near Ormesby, a thatched church with a ruined round tower, used as a barn. When Faden published his map of the county in 1797 he recorded 'Ormesby Old Church in ruins', as did the Ordnance Survey in 1838. Nowadays nothing above ground remains.

The crop-mark clearly shows the round tower, the nave with buttresses, the chancel and the central division. There is also a fainter mark of an earlier apsidal (rounded) east end, superceded by the rectangular chancel. This suggests that the church was of Saxon or Norman build, with the chancel later extended.

The road on which Blomefield travelled is represented by the sinuous white crop-mark ending at the allotment fence behind the church site. It was diverted in 1842 to the present course visible in the top left hand corner. The dark lines mark the boundaries of old fields and plots, apparently of early date though their exact age cannot be told.

The two fields to north and south of Ryston church contain one of the last good examples of ridge and furrow left in the county. The individual ridges usually correspond to medieval strip fields and these were grouped together into blocks of strip fields called 'furlongs'. In the Midlands ridge and furrow is still fairly common, but in East Anglia their survival is now very rare indeed. In Norfolk most of the recorded examples are in the west of the county; there is an excellent set at Hilgay, between the Hilgay bypass and the village, clearly visible from the A10 trunk road.

The ridge and furrow in this picture belonged to the deserted village of Ryston, which was mentioned in Domesday Book and survived the Black Death (it was granted tax relief in 1352 to cover the effects of the plague) but had gone by the eighteenth century. Only the Norman church survives, though its unusual tower is a rebuild of 1858. The village was probably deliberately removed to form the park of Ryston Hall, which formerly comprised all the land on the left-hand side of the photograph. The hall was built by Sir Roger Pratt around 1670.

Hill Farm and the houses behind it (background) are in Denver parish. Since this photograph was taken a new bypass around Denver has been driven left to right between the church and the farm, bisecting Elf Wood (centre).

In an outlying part of the old parish of Hapton, now part of Tharston, there is a rare survival of a group of strip fields still being cultivated separately. The shape of these fields, following a 'reversed S', is very characteristic of medieval strips. This shape was formed gradually over the centuries by the turning of the plough at the headland. These strips, which are themselves amalgamations of two or three medieval strips, give some indication of how the countryside would have looked in the Middle Ages. The origin of this system is unclear, although it is presumably Anglo-Saxon; it was the usual method of parcelling cultivated land until gradual amalgamation and enclosure became widespread from the fifteenth century onwards. Old parish maps from the sixteenth, seventeenth and eighteenth centuries frequently show the open field system gradually being replaced by hedged fields. This enclosure movement culminated in the nineteenth century with the parcelling up of the commons and heaths, the areas of common grazing which had been kept quite separate from the cultivated strips.

For many people who visit Norfolk each year for their holidays, Norfolk is synonymous with the Broads. To Norfolk people this is surprising because these open stretches of water do actually cover a very small part of the Norfolk scene and they are difficult to appreciate except by boat. The origins of the Broads remained undiscovered until the early 1950s despite the plentiful existence of medieval documents which revealed their purpose. They had been thought to represent a discontinuous pattern of natural lakes left behind as the sea retreated from the eastern valleys after they had been flooded in Roman times. Then, significant studies involving the investigation of soil samples taken from bore-holes made through the valley deposits and the deposits of the Broads themselves showed that they are man-made pits dug for the extraction of peat. At the same time documentary historians working on records, such as those of Norwich Cathedral Priory, showed that these peat diggings or 'turbaries' were well established in the twelfth century and continued production until the fourteenth century. In its heyday turf cutting was a thriving industry providing domestic fuel and possibly also fuel for salt-working along the east coast. However, by the fourteenth century extraction was becoming progressively more difficult as the pits flooded due to increasing rainfall and rising sea level.

This 1952 photograph of Barton Broad is especially interesting as it shows peninsulas and patches of reed in lines running across the Broad since removed by dredging. These lines, six of which can be seen in the foreground, mark the positions of submerged baulks of undisturbed peat demarcating different holdings on strips (as in **57**) over which people had rights within the peat digging areas. The parish name comes from the digging of 'turves'.*

The Old Podyke, Marshland St James

TF 553 052

In the thirteenth century, Marshland, the silt region between King's Lynn and Wisbech bordering the Wash, was one of the richest regions in Norfolk. Not only were there extensive tracts of marsh which could be reclaimed for cultivation, but also areas of rich summer pasture for grazing stock. Of these the most important was West Fen, a large area of peat on the southern edge of Marshland. The siltland villages had rights of common pasturage on West Fen as well as the right to cut peat in spring, a vital source of fuel in a region where wood was in short supply. So important was the fen that when, in the early thirteenth century, the risk of fresh water flooding from the uplands became acute, the villages of Walpole, Terrington, Tilney, West Walton and others grouped together to construct a protective barrier along the southern side. Thus, in 1223 a bank with an outer ditch, the Old Podyke, came into existence. It functioned until 1422 when, breached so many times by floods, it was considered to be beyond repair and was replaced by the New Podyke (**117**) further to the south. Nevertheless, the Old Podyke survives today as a sinuous feature in a landscape dominated by the geometric layout of fields, droves and roads resulting from the enclosure of common land in the late eighteenth century. In places the bank has been levelled off and is now cultivated (as in the foreground of the photograph). However, one or two short stretches still survive to a height of over 2m (as in the middle distance), providing a vivid impression of what this medieval flood defence must once have looked like.

Baconsthorpe is more of a fortified manor house than a castle, and as such is one of Norfolk's best examples after Oxborough (**61**). The moated site beside the great fishpond was originally that of Wood Hall Manor. Between 1480 and 1486 the present inner gatehouse and part of the encircling walls were built; three stages of development were needed to bring the island layout to its present form. The outer gatehouse (right) was an even later addition of 1560, flanked by its pepperpot turrets. By this time fortification was out of fashion; the new building was designed for show and the old sections became a wool processing factory – the top left hand tower of the inner circuit contains a steeping tank, just visible. The barn, whose roof appears in the bottom right hand corner of the photograph, also dates from this period, though altered.

In 1600 the drawbridge entrance and facade were altered to give a more impressive appearance, but this attempt at reinstating the older section did not last long; in 1654 loads of stone were carried away to build Felbrigg Hall, whereas the outer gatehouse was given a new porch tower (removed in 1820) and became known as Baconsthorpe Hall. It was the only inhabited section until 1920, when one tower collapsed without warning. The site was then abandoned until stabilisation of the ruins was begun by the then Ministry of Works in 1953, followed by excavation of the silted moat.*

Oxburgh represents the ideal moated house to many people. Towering above its fish-filled moat and surrounded by park and gardens, it is the perfect English stately home.

Licence to construct a fortified dwelling was obtained from the Crown in 1482 – after the work had been completed. The grand gatehouse remains unaltered from this time, and contains one of the few genuine priest's holes in Norfolk. Three sides of the courtyard are basically original, including the roofs; the east (right hand) range originally contained a first floor open hall. The fourth side of the quadrangle, opposite the gatehouse, contained the Great Hall, regrettably demolished in 1775. The south-east (far right hand) corner of the building was burnt down in the Civil War and not repaired until 1725.

In 1830 a thorough campaign of 'regothicisation' took place, adding new dormers, pinnacles, oriels and bay windows, following on from the provision of the single storey corridor around the courtyard. The work culminated in 1838 in the raising of the great south-east tower. The foreground building was once the base of an even larger south-west tower, since reduced. The walls and towers of the kitchen garden in the right background were part of these works.

The hall is now the property of the National Trust but is still inhabited by the Bedingfeld family, whose ancestors were its original builders. *

The surprising fact about Hales Hall is that the impressive buildings that remain are only the outer service court. The actual hall stood to the left of the photograph, where the base of one tower can be seen in the remaining angle of the moat. Originally founded in the thirteenth century by the De Hales family (it is in fact just over the border of Hales parish into Loddon) it was rebuilt in about 1510 by Sir James Hobart and inhabited until about 1740.

The remaining outer courtyard, which was once moated, is believed to have been built as part of this same scheme. The Great Barn (foreground) is one of the longest in the county; its right hand end, as can be seen from the windows, comprises two-storeyed living accommodation. The roof, with its queenpost above the barn and with crownposts added over the living quarters, was formerly thatched. The wall containing the gateway connects it with the domestic range, including the north gateway at the left-hand end, which is now the main house. The small building at the right-hand end beyond the wall, built across the line of the moat, appears to be a seventeenth-century cottage built with older materials.

A track across Hales Green approached the hall from the right, and until recently the public footpath continued through the gateway to meet a bridle path coming through the north gatehouse. The original entrance road from Loddon came in from the top left of the photograph, and was for long the only passable road to the town in winter.*

Mannington Hall seems dwarfed by its watery surroundings in this view, the encircling moat being separated by only a narrow island from the lake in the foreground formed by widening a tributary of the river Bure. The hall was under construction in 1460, was altered in the sixteenth century and greatly changed in 1864 – the latter including eccentricities such as an inscription 'A tiger is something worse than a snake, a demon than a tiger, a woman than a demon, and nothing worse than a woman' and other sentiments thankfully in Latin. The south front (left foreground), part of the original work of 1460, has two projecting turrets containing the staircase, garderobes (toilets) and a reputed priest's hole of later date. These are at the end of the Great Hall, which has since been divided up. The adjoining block to the right is of 1864. At the rear of the latter, the lower building running down to the moat is the original kitchen. The range of buildings behind it date from 1864 but stand on older foundations.

The right-hand bridge to the island is of sixteenth- or seventeenth-century brickwork, but the left-hand bridge is a metal drawbridge of 1864 and now a listed building in its own right. In the small garden building beside it were recently discovered a large number of slabs of Oland stone from Sweden, believed to have been originally imported for Sir Christopher Wren and no doubt acquired as a bargain by a previous owner of the hall, but never used.

West Barsham Old Hall, Barsham

TF 904 333

These earthworks at West Barsham were first noted by an American airman in 1955, and were believed to be the remains of a deserted village. It was not until 1979 that it was realised they constitute a formal garden layout. The canalised stream, with a central pond, runs through the centre of the photograph, and is parallelled on each side by a bank and ditch halfway up the slope of a shallow valley. To the left, the rectangular banked area appears to be a raised knot garden (a formal garden surrounded by an earthwork bank within which flower beds were separated by dwarf hedges in the form of knots). The other earthworks probably represent garden beds and walks. At the bottom left is a large mound by the source of the stream, known locally as the 'burial mound', though it does not appear to be such. Mounds like these had their origin in monastery gardens, and passed into Elizabethan and Jacobean layouts where they were designed to give a view from the formal garden over the 'untamed' outside world. Sometimes they bore a summerhouse or belvedere. The small house at the extreme right of the nearer group of buildings is the remaining fragment of the Old Hall, supposedly a Jacobean house burnt down in 1812. The garden plan probably belongs to this hall in its original form. In the background is the present Hall, built in the 1940s on the site of another house.

Between the two groups of buildings can be seen West Barsham church (with central porch). This is a beautifully maintained little church of Saxo-Norman date; the church once had a central tower and there are Roman tiles in the fabric.

Blickling Hall

TG 179 284

Blickling has been owned by the National Trust since 1940 when it received the estate totalling 4,500 acres as a bequest at the death of the 11th Marquess of Lothian. The hall and the park are both open to the public. The house dates largely from the period 1619 to 1625 when it was rebuilt by Sir Henry Hobart to designs prepared by Robert Lyminge. The north and west fronts were rebuilt in the eighteenth century. Humphrey Repton was responsible for replanting the park and enlarging the lake at the end of the eighteenth century. The picture shows the east face as designed by Lyminge, and in front of that the remains of a once-elaborate parterre garden laid out in 1872. Although most of these flower beds were removed in 1930 they can still be seen in this picture showing through the lawn which at the time the picture was taken was suffering from drought. The Woodland Garden, built up on a terrace, is apparently seventeenth century in origin, although it was developed later with an eighteenth-century Doric Temple at the end of the main walk.

The estate was recorded accurately by William Corbridge who drew a plan of the area in 1729; with this and later maps it is possible to study how the park has evolved over the last two and a half centuries.*

The massive bulk of Houghton Hall is an alien intrusion into the Norfolk landscape. Even the stone used to build it came from Aislaby in Yorkshire; nobody had brought in stone from that far afield in Britain except perhaps the Romans to clad Brancaster fort (**21**). It was erected in 1722-35 near the site of an older mansion, in a derivative of the Palladian style by Colen Campbell and Thomas Ripley, for Britain's first prime minister, Sir Robert Walpole. The effect of the *piano nobile* or formal first floor rooms raised above the ground floor intended for 'hunters, hospitality, noise, dirt and business' was somewhat lost by the removal of the external stone entrance stairs in the late eighteenth century. Happily the flanking wings survive, though the right hand one is nowadays largely a shell. The detached stable block of the same date, with beautiful red brick vaulting, would elswhere make a mansion in itself (far left).

Even the landscape was altered (by Bridgeman) to an artificial appearance. The house stands at the intersection of four sunken avenues, known as Views, as if its weight were depressing the ground. To achieve the appearance of formal isolation the village had to go (**67**) from the site where it had stood since Domesday Book – though it had already been partly depopulated in 1517. Its earthworks can be glimpsed in the trees behind the church, which strangely enough was not demolished although in a poor state of repair. Instead, the building of the fourteenth century and 1513 was restored and given a new tower. The village cross was also allowed to remain, though in a new position; it is hidden by the tree just above the pond.*

The old village of Houghton was probably demolished during the late 1720s. In 1729 a new village was laid out on a fresh site beyond the new park fence about half a kilometre due south of the new house. The original plan of the village shows five double cottages on either side of a new road. Each unit comprised a large front living-room with fireplace and oven and a smaller back room, with bedrooms above. The central pair on each side of the road had back rooms of a slighly greater depth than the other pairs. Subsequent alterations and additions transformed at least two of the cottages into four-family dwellings, and lean-to outshuts and outbuildings were added both before and after 1800. The low buildings at right angles to the road at the extreme left were almshouses, built after 1838, and the school (out of the picture to the left) was built in 1845. Hall Farm (just off the picture at the top left corner) was built in the 1730s as the New Inn; subsequently its name was changed to the King's Head, and it became Hall Farm c. 1840. Until the late eighteenth century the main entrance to the park was between a pair of lodges opposite the New Inn. The present entrance at the north end of the village street was created by the 4th Earl of Cholmondeley c. 1798 -1800, using gates brought from Cholmondeley Hall, Cheshire. Village Farm, just off the right edge of the picture, was built at the same time as the New Inn. The village is now a conservation area.

The space between the ranks of trees to the left of the picture is an extension, c. 1730, of the South View from the Hall (**66**).

The future of this fine building, which has stood empty for many years, is at last looking brighter. Both the architect and the exact date of erection are unknown; a previous hall which stood on the site was in process of demolition in 1664 and a ceiling in the present building is dated 1687. The building is very much in the style of Sir Roger Pratt, the Norfolk architect who built Ryston Hall for himself; yet it also shows the influence of the new Netherlandish style being introduced at the time by architects such as Sir Christopher Wren and his circle. The result is a near-perfect example of the Domestic Classical style – 'near' because a cupola on the roof has been removed. It is shown on the architect's model now in the Norfolk Rural Life Museum. Happily, an overbearing Victorian north addition of 1850 has been removed. There have been other small additions – the colonnade (foreground) was added in 1757, somewhat spoiling the symmetry, and the terraces are of 1856, but the south front seen from the park still gives an unrivalled appearance. The stable court beyond the house, though containing some seventeenth-century brickwork, is mostly of 1810; the block linking it to the hall was refaced in 1887 and extended to the right in 1926.

The interior of the mansion has some magnificent ceilings with plaster birds and flowers as pendants and reliefs, which were apparently made by a craftsman who also worked at Felbrigg Hall and Hintlesham in Suffolk.

The present hall was erected for Sir Jacob Astley, then a young man in his twenties. The site passed in direct male succession from 1236 until its sale by the 20th Lord Hastings in 1956.

The desire of the eighteenth-century gentry to surround their houses with acres of parkland is best demonstrated in Norfolk at Holkham. Such parks may appear to us to be natural, but in reality they were carefully planned and contrived.

Holkham Park illustrates several phases of development. The hall and the original park were planned as one, and even before the building of the hall began the first structure in the park was erected in 1727. This was the obelisk, seen here in the wooded area in the centre of the photograph. It stands at the highest point in the park and it would have been the focal point for visitors as they came up the straight 2.5 km avenue from the Triumphal Arch (just off the photograph). The centre of the house was then aligned on the obelisk to the south and on two lodge houses (now demolished and replaced in 1845 by a monument to the agriculturalist, Thomas William Coke) to the north. The monument can just be seen in the trees.

The house itself, built for Thomas Coke, uncle of the agriculturalist, was designed by William Kent, Matthew Brettingham and Coke himself. It was begun in 1734 and is a very fine example of the Palladian style of architecture.

To the left of the house is the lake. A dam was built in 1727 at the seaward end of this muddy depression; the lake is fed naturally by several springs. In 1803 the ends were curved to give it a more natural appearance and the islands were redesigned in the 1840s. The latest alterations to the area around the house were made in the 1850s when the terrace gardens were created.*

The original hall was built in 1606 by Sir Thomas Holland, an MP who made his name as an opponent of James I's arbitrary rule. His descendants continued in the family traditions and were strong supporters of Oliver Cromwell. All that remains externally of this house are a few mullioned windows and two turrets not visible in this photograph. Inside, however, there is a remarkable moulded ceiling above the staircase dated 1619 and showing Noah's Ark full of animals and upheld by the Hand of God. The Jacobean architect's model for the original building is on display in the Norfolk Rural Life Museum.

When the male line of the Holland family died out the house was bought by the 3rd Earl of Albermarle in 1762 and he undertook many alterations to the building. The most impressive facade to the west is not visible in this view, but the garden front can be seen to the left with its recessed Tuscan porch, possibly the last section to be remodelled.

The Albermarles were close friends of the Cokes of Holkham and, like them, were staunch supporters of the Whig cause. Like many other Whigs, their belief in 'liberty' meant they welcomed the French Revolution, and Lord Albermarle hung a portrait of Napoleon over his bed 'and regarded it much in the light of a patron saint'!

In 1802 the interiors were altered by C. Heathcote Tatham; all that survives of this is the drawing room ceiling and the beautiful library, in the Corinthian style. Pediments were added to the ground floor windows (foreground) in 1892.

The house remained in the Albermarle family until 1948; then it became a Carmelite monastery, which has about thirty nuns at present. The cloisters, chapter room, public chapel and bell tower were added in the 1950s. To the right, stables have been converted into a guest house and behind that is a print shop where the nuns run printing presses.

Elsing Hall TG 039 160

Appearances are deceptive in this view of Elsing Hall. Despite its 'Olde Englande' appearance, virtually all the exterior of this ancient building is less than 150 years old. It stands within a medieval moat; the island was once ringed with walls and towers, of which some foundations remain. In the trees to the left is a fishpond. The hall itself can be dated to 1436-77 by the heraldry of John Hastings carved on the porch (on the side further from the camera), and may include older walling. In 1852 Thomas Jekyll 'restored' the building and remade almost all of the outer walls, certainly that of the south front seen here, as paintings of the hall by Thomas Bulwer around 1830 prove. The two projecting timber-framed wings which formerly had eighteenth-century Venetian windows were rebuilt, the section between them brought forward, outbuildings to the left demolished, and plain chimneys replaced by ornate examples. Yet the plan of the house is basically unchanged, an H-shape with the chapel projecting on the right, and the kitchen wing on the left slightly recessed from the entrance front to avoid spoiling the symmetry. Inside, the open hall survives, with bay window and stair turret, though much restored. Thus, despite its external remaking, the house is still an important survival of medieval architecture.

The small building at the extreme left of the block, screened by trees, is a set of latrines emptying into the moat; a medieval practice though the latrines were not erected until after 1830.

The story of the building of Bylaugh Hall is a strange one. The Lombe family did not originate in Norfolk, but made their fortunes as silk manufacturers in Derby. They began buying Norfolk estates in the early eighteenth century and acquired the six hundred acres at Bylaugh as payment for a gambling debt in 1796.

When Sir John Lombe died in 1817, he gave instructions in his will that a hall should be constructed at Bylaugh, and over the principal entrance is the inscription 'Ex Jussu Curiae Cancellariae' (erected by the order of Chancery).

It is not often that a country house was built on an entirely new site on 'what a few years back was only a Turnip field' (*Norwich Mercury* 1851). It was designed by Messrs. Barry and Banks (Mr Barry was the son of Sir Charles, the architect of the Houses of Parliament) and work began in 1849. The house was one of the first to be built with steel girders to strengthen it, which helps to explain why the ruin has survived so well. No expense was spared and even contemporaries felt that 'It was a little overdone with sugar loaves of stone.' The problem was that all the money set aside for its building and held by the court of Chancery had to be spent and this resulted in the creation of a sumptuous house and grounds. It had a magnificent saloon 'which had a panel carved roof and plaques finely modelled in alto relivo in white and gold'. When the house was completed the trustees went back to Chancery, but not all the money had been used, so the clock tower was built and gardens planted, but there was still money left over. Finally the lodges were erected and the park was surrounded by a 14km wall by 1852.

Mr Lombe, for whom it was built, was an elderly gentleman, not well enough to move in, and none of his successors liked the house, so it was hardly ever used. They had been forced to build it to inherit, and may well have resented the extravagance. It was sold with difficulty in 1917 and still was mostly unoccupied until finally, in 1950, the interior was demolished and it was reduced to the shell as seen in the photograph.

Sandringham House TF 694 287 ◄●

Like Bylaugh (**72**), Sandringham is a creation of the Victorian era, but unlike it, the site was not a new one, and the building of the house involved the partial demolition of an older one, newly altered for the previous owner by the flamboyant Victorian architect Samuel Teulon.

The estate was bought by HRH Prince of Wales in 1862 and he immediately planned to alter the house. Only Teulon's conservatory remains, converted into a billiard room, with a bowling alley alongside it. The present house was designed by A.J. Humbert and was completed in 'Jacobethan' style in 1870. The house has been little altered since then, except for restoration after a fire in 1891 and the demolition of an extensive wing in 1975.

The formal gardens reflect late nineteenth-century taste while the extent of the woodland in the background reminds us that this is the focus of one of the country's foremost shooting estates.

The house is owned by the Queen, and the royal family usually spends some of the New Year holiday on the estate.*

This seventeenth-century house sits within an irregularly-shaped medieval moat and is flanked by a range of nineteenth-century farm buildings. The site is that of a manor house, the manor being created in the twelfth century; but the scale is that of a typical south Norfolk farmhouse. This area of the country on relatively flat ill-drained clay is characterised by numerous small farms, frequently with a timber-framed house of sixteenth-or seventeenth-century date, dotted around the edges of large, often linear, greens. That these properties were already old by the time the present houses were built is often indicated by the encircling moats, first dug in the thirteenth or fourteenth centuries. This pattern is in marked contrast to much of the north and west of the county where large eighteenth-century estates and new agricultural methods produced a far more uniform and open landscape (**24**). Heywood manor lies close to the parish boundary with Winfarthing near the northern end of an extraordinary extension, *c.* 5 km by 1 km, of Diss Parish, named the Heywood. Within this area are eight other moated sites. Of these, one, Heywood Hall, was manorial, and the other seven were farms, of which five survive as dwellings to the present day.

The Great Barn at Waxham Hall appears in a sorry state in this 1983 photograph, its right hand end virtually unroofed since a thatcher employed in restoration earlier this century fell from it, leaving the work uncompleted. It may surprise many Norfolk inhabitants to know that this barn is longer and wider (53.3 m by 8.2 m) than the more famous example at Paston and is important in that, unlike Paston and other large barns, it is still part of a manorial complex, though this is not apparent on the photograph. It is set in part of a walled enclosure which also includes the remaining two wings of the hall (off the photograph at top) and one of two outer gateways. The parish church is just off the picture to the right, outside this enclosure, and there is a tradition that the barn was once used as a tithe barn.

The barn is built of flint with brick diaperwork (diamond patterning) and has buttresses containing re-used limestone from a church – the property is said to have once belonged to Hickling Priory, though all the present buildings seem to belong to the late sixteenth century. The roof is composed of alternate hammerbeams and queenposts, similar to Paston Barn and a barn at Godwick. The builder is thought to be Sir Thomas Woodhouse, who died in 1571 and is buried in the church.

A human skull was once found under the threshold: its story is unknown.

The 'cotton reels' in the foreground are 'big bales' of straw; this recent farming innovation involves wrapping straw tightly into large bales which are sufficiently waterproof to be stored out of doors.

This very large and impressive set of farm buildings at Waterden Farm illustrates the phases of Norfolk agriculture in the 100 years after 1760. It was part of the forty-thousand acre estate owned by Thomas William Coke, later Earl of Leicester of Holkham, famous for his interest in agricultural progress and the improving of farm buildings.

These premises were built to serve a farm of 750 acres and the oldest building is the huge central L-shaped barn which would have originally contained four threshing floors. These were placed between double doors so that the draught when the doors were open would blow away the chaff as the grain was being hand-threshed with the flail. Dating from the period in the nineteenth century when grain was the most valuable crop on the farm, these great barns are an indication of the agricultural wealth created during the Napoleonic Wars.

The first description of these buildings was written by the agricultural journalist Arthur Young in 1784: 'Every convenience to be imagined is thought of and the offices so perfectly well arranged as to answer the great object; to prevent waste and save labour'. In 1816, they were described as 'perhaps the finest set of farm premises in Great Britain.'

The E-shaped sets of cattle sheds shown on the photograph were built in 1871 but almost certainly replace earlier ones on the same site. They were built to the south of the barn to provide warmth and shelter and would have housed about 50 cattle. Foreign imports of cheap grain by the late 1870s meant that it was livestock rather than wheat which was the most valuable product of the farm, while with the introduction of threshing machinery, the barn with its threshing floors became obsolete. The other buildings included stable and workshops.

Situated just to the south of Holkham park, Branthill Farm is one of the show-pieces of the Holkham estate. It was a light-land farm and like others on these poorer soils, was very large, extending to about 1,000 acres in the nineteenth century. To farm these soils successfully they needed careful attention and plenty of manure so, by 1851 the cattle sheds on the south (warm) side of the barn had been built to house sixty cattle. There were also stables for twenty-five horses. The barn is a very large one, even for the Holkham estate, renowned as it was for the size of its barns. There are two sets of double doors, with porches on the south side. Between these sets of doors would have been the threshing floors.

In the foreground is the substantial yellow brick farmhouse and beside it a cottage, originally built not only for the steward and his family, but also to lodge six or seven team men (the farm workers responsible for a team of horses each). Even by the standards of the mid-nineteenth century, it was thought to be really too small for all these people.

This is a fine example of a Holkham farmstead, surviving nearly intact on the edge of the park.

Rural poverty was a major problem in Norfolk in the second half of the eighteenth century. Traditionally the poor had been looked after in their own parishes but then, in several areas of the county, the major landowners combined to obtain a private Act of Parliament to group their parishes into 'Incorporations' to build large 'Houses of Industry'. The house of industry at Gressenhall was built in 1776-7 to accommodate the poor of the incorporated parishes within the hundreds of Mitford and Launditch. The building was planned with an original H-shaped blocked with two L-shaped wings to either side. However, because the number of inmates was lower than anticipated the west wing was never built.

The style of the buildings was described as 'plain and durable', yet the pediment on the front, containing the clock, and the attractive cupola above, where the bell which governed the working hours of the inmates hung, gives the central building a certain classical elegance often lacking in later institutions. The inmates worked in the surrounding fields (which also belonged to the incorporation) growing food for consumption in the house or for sale, or were employed at spinning. Later, a sack factory was established on the premises.

The Poor Law Amendment Act of 1834 enforced a harsher approach to poor relief and in 1836 major changes took place at Gressenhall. The old 'House of Industry' became a 'Union Workhouse' serving a slightly larger area than before. The boundary wall, a porter's lodge and most of the single storey range on the left of the photograph were erected, together with internal walls, to ensure the proper segregation of different classes of inmates. Married couples could no longer live together and this involved alteration to the original buildings.

The chapel (by R.M. Phipson) was added in 1868, and the cottage running parallel to the outside wall near the bottom of the picture was built as a fever ward in 1871. The long low structure near the top of the picture was erected as a steam laundry in 1902. In 1930 the workhouse became a 'public assistance institution' and subsequently an old people's home until it was transferred to the Norfolk Museums Service in 1976. It now houses the Norfolk Rural Life Museum and the Norfolk Archaeological Unit.*

Pulham Market workhouse TM 185 875

The Depwade Union workhouse at Pulham differs from Gressenhall workhouse in that the main buildings date from 1836-7. The architect, William Thorold, a 'cunning man' in the words of the Assistant Poor Law Commissioner, Dr James Kay, helped to persuade the Board of Guardians to erect a larger and more expensive structure than they had originally contemplated; accommodation for 400 inmates was provided at a cost of £9,700. The plan was symmetrical, with a central octagonal building housing the dining hall linked to an outer octagon by four large wings terminated by pedimented gables. Parts of this original plan have been destroyed in twentieth century alterations and, as at Gressenhall, internal dividing walls in the yards have been removed. The whole was surrounded by another wall, much of which survives, creating an almost square enclosure, with turrets at the corners. In correspondence with Dr Kay, the Board of Guardians stressed the necessity of this wall; it is said to have been erected in response to the damage caused by local poor, infuriated by the prospect of incarceration in the bastille which they saw rising before their eyes; but since it was included in the original plans, the depredations must have been anticipated. The hostility of the poor necessitated the employment of two policemen in the summer of 1837 while the building was being completed, and several years later was expressed again in an unsuccessful attempt to burn it down. Today, as an hotel, it provides hospitality on a somewhat more lavish scale for travellers on the A140 Norwich to Ipswich trunk road.

The original settlement at East Dereham was probably around the Norman church, at top right with its tall freestanding belltower of 1501-36. Immediately left of this can be seen the thatched roof of Bishop Bonner's Cottages, dated 1502, beyond what was once one of the the manor houses. The medieval town probably spread from the guildhall (rebuilt in the eighteenth century – at top centre in the trees) to the High Street (upper left).

However two disastrous fires swept the town in 1581 and 1679, and it has been suggested that the market place (centre, with parked cars) was laid out on virgin ground after the first fire, as happened at Watton in the same period. It originally extended back as far as Church Street (beyond its present left-hand end) and Quebec Street (above it in the photograph), the present three islands of buildings marking encroachments on the sites of market stalls, probably before 1679. The result was the present shape – the right-hand area (with war memorial) until recent years being the cattle market.

A general rebuilding and refacing of the houses around the Market Place was carried out around 1756. The building on the left-hand side of the right-hand island is the Assembly House of that date, on the site of a lockup, pound and Town House.

The nineteenth century saw the Corn Hall added in 1857 at the far left-hand end of the large island and the Cowper Memorial Chapel (centre left) built by Boardman in 1873 on the site of the house where the poet died. The inns that once stood around the market place have all now gone, and the new post office (centre right-hand margin) replaced Becclesgate House, a fine Georgian mansion.*

Swaffham market place grew up at the crossing point of the main east-to-west Norwich to King's Lynn road and the north-to-south Fakenham to Brandon road. The de Sabaudin family who were lords of the manor in the thirteenth century encouraged trade so successfully that by the mid-thirteenth century there were two weekly markets. Unlike many other medieval markets, Swaffham continued to prosper in the years after the Black Death. Its magnificent church to the east of the market place was re-built in the late fifteenth century when other centres were already in decline.

By the eighteenth century it was a fashionable centre with a race-course on the heath, assembly rooms and a theatre. It was an important staging point for coaches and it supported several coaching inns. Many of the older houses were given fashionable Georgian facades. At the south end of the market place is the elegant butter market with a statue of Ceres, goddess of the harvest, on the dome. It was erected by the Earl of Orford in 1783.

To the north is another building reminding us of the agricultural wealth of the region. The Romanesque brick corn hall was built in 1858. It contained a billiard-room and library downstairs. Upstairs was a large room occupied by corn merchants on market day and also used for concerts, lectures, and other public events. It is now the Job Centre.

On Saturday this fine triangular market place hosts one of Norfolk's ancient markets, full of stalls with a small livestock auction as well, attended by those buying and selling poultry, rabbits and goats.*

The town of Burnham Market is a relatively recent creation, being a combination of Burnham Westgate, Burnham Ulph and Burnham Sutton – three of the 'Seven Burnhams by the Sea', though the sites of at least two other churches are covered by the present town. This view encompasses Burnham Westgate, around the former market place – across which the Goose Beck flows in wet weather. St Mary's church contains traces of a Norman building but is mostly fourteenth- and fifteenth-century work; it has remarkable carved battlements. To its right only the roof is visible of Westgate Hall, rebuilt in 1783 by De Carle to a design of Sir John Soane for Lord Camelford; its former park stretches away beyond. The houses round the market place have eighteenth-century exteriors, some on older cores; that at centre right with dormers is the Hoste Arms public house, commemorating one of Norfolk's lesser known heroes, Sir William Hoste, one of Nelson's captains. In the foreground more recent housing has spread over former backlands along Station Road.*

Like a great black hole, the mere at Diss seems about to swallow the town in this photograph. The H-shaped settlement, strung out along Mere Street (to right) St Nicholas Street – Market Hill (top) and Denmark Street (left), with more recent backland encroachment, grew up around and takes its name from the lake (Saxon 'dic' meaning ditch, pond or watercourse). There is evidence that the mere once extended even further towards the bottom right hand corner of the photograph.

The oldest part of the settlement is probably centred on the market place, below the church at the top of Mere Street. The church dates mostly from around 1300, with later additions; what may have been ancient cremation burials found beneath it in 1773 suggest that it might represent a consecration of a pagan site. Just in front of it on the right hand side of the market place is Dolphin House, a fine jettied early seventeenth-century building. Above the top centre of the mere in St Nicholas Street can be seen the pedimented portico of the Corn Hall of 1854 by the local architect George Atkin. Adjoining it on the right is the Greyhound Inn, a sixteenth-century building with elaborate interiors remade in the reign of James II.

Denmark Street mainly consists of later buildings than the other two main thoroughfares, though the rectangle of maltings at top left built in 1788 stand on the site of a moated mansion. Between the road and the mere can be seen the Baptist Chapel with its twin towers, a well-known local landmark.*

The 'Ancient Capital of East Anglia', as Leigh Hunt called it, is centred on the junction of the rivers Little Ouse and Thet which emerge from the shelter of wooded islands to join and pass under the bridge. The Little Ouse formed the county boundary until 1870. 'Thetford' means 'the ford used by many people' and takes its names from the river crossing of the Icknield Way, protected by an Iron Age fort later used as a Norman castle, just visible bottom left (**15**). Having been occupied by the Danes in 870 AD, the town became of great importance in Late Saxon and early medieval times – at one point having twenty-four churches – but then it began to decline. The area of the southern (further) bank of the river was largely abandoned; the playing fields towards top centre are within the Saxon town, whose boundary is marked by the line of trees along their further edge.

At top right can be seen the ruins of St Mary's Cluniac priory, founded in 1103 and moved to this site in 1114, mostly rebuilt after upgrading from an alien cell (a dependency of a foreign monastry) in 1376. The buildings to the left of the river between the old bridge and the relief road bridge comprise the Grammar School, a former religious house which for a time acted as the cathedral before removal of the bishop of East Anglia to Norwich in 1094-6, and afterwards became a Dominican friary. Fragments of Late Saxon carved stonework are incorporated in the school buildings.

In the present century Thetford has begun to recolonise the southern bank, with the Newtown and St Mary's estates of the 1950s (centre left) and the Redcastle Furze estate of the 1960s (top centre), part of the London Overspill Plan.*

The Saturday Market Place and St Margaret's Church were the focus of the original Lynn in the twelfth century: the market was the key to the development of trade, under the watchful eye of its ecclesiastical patrons, represented by the small daughter house of Benedictines at St Margaret's. The shadow cast by St Margaret's towers over the market place on the photograph had a real substance then! Note the curve of Queen Street (centre left), at that time on the edge of the water, which later receded west. College Lane, running down by the quadrangle of Thoresby College, was one of the few public access points to the river once this happened, for the space between bank and street became filled with the merchants' own warehouses and wharves. The South Quay, along which the cars are parked, is a twentieth-century addition. Prominent in the market place is the Trinity Guildhall (1419-20), most important of the medieval merchant guilds and annual supplier of the candidate for Mayor, hence its continuing association with the post-dissolution corporation. Behind it the enormous car park represents the 1960s clearance of the former densely-packed yards to make a servicing area for the pedestrianisation of the High Street, which in medieval times housed the tradesmen, just as Queen Street did the merchants.*

Until the nineteenth century Purfleet was an important waterway, lined with wharves at the rivermost end and an important sewer upstream. In the late nineteenth century it was partially covered over, leaving only the stretch below High Street visible. Readily choked with mud, until comparatively recent times a nearby firm kept the river entry clear for their own use. By 1986 it was completely choked, but was cleared out for use in the film 'Revolution' as seen here. The imitation (but convincing!) frontages of the film set and the presence of sail gave Lynn a glimpse of its former busy character. McConnahay's warehouse camouflaged the grain silos which have taken the place of a former old warehouse. Much disliked by those who remember their predecessor, when in use the silos nevertheless gave a striking impression of the working conjunction of old and new, not entirely unpleasing. Now derelict, their increasing dilapidation does not have the picturesqueness of traditional buildings in similar circumstances. Beside the bridge, Henry Bell's Custom House of 1683, with its Dutch influence, lent authenticity to this recreation of eighteenth-century New York.*

The Bentinck Dock, crossing the picture from left to right, was opened as an extension to the earlier Alexandra Dock in 1883. It was formerly lined with massive brick warehouses whose overwhelming impression of strength owed much to their intrinsically plain and simple proportions. The last of these came down in 1973 to make room for the tall concrete silo, now the tallest building in the town. On the right is the swing bridge over the narrow channel into the outer dock, and immediately below, bordering the road over it, the Fisher Fleet. This channel, opening directly onto the river, shelters the small fishing boats whose main business is with shrimps and shellfish. Until the re-cutting of the course of the river in the 1860s, to enter the Wash further west, the whole area of this photograph was part of the bed of the Great Ouse.

Just east of the Roman fort at Brancaster (**21**) is the Staithe (landing place), one of a line of medieval harbours strung out along the north-Norfolk coast, protected from the open sea by salt-marsh and mudflats; many have now silted up and the ports declined. The staithe is at the head of a long channel, winding in from the sea behind the long shingle bank of Scolt Head, a sheltered haven for the sailing boats which bring the area alive in summer.

In the Middle Ages Ramsey Abbey in the fens held the manor of Brancaster and claimed extensive rights here. The abbot had a special court to control the harbour and protect his rights over anchorage and his claim to wrecks and fish cast up by the sea.

The staithe was a good local harbour and remained in use after the abbey lost control of Brancaster in the sixteenth century; some larger houses (top left), of seventeenth and eighteenth century origins, may reflect continuing trade. In the eighteenth century a remarkable malthouse was built (some say the largest in England), using stone from the Roman fort. Disused by the mid-nineteenth century, its site is among the trees (left); its quay survives at the end of the lane.

However, in 1845 a large trade in coal and corn still helped support three public houses, including The Jolly Sailors, as well as a school-master, a milliner and two draper/grocers!

More recently, the staithe has been a centre for the mussel industry and mussel cleansing pits can be seen in the foreground. It is now a peaceful haven for holidaymakers, in a designated Area of Outstanding Natural Beauty.*

Deserted by the sea, the ancient port of Cley is visited now by tourists. They come to see its famous windmill (foreground), old houses with tiled roofs and 'Dutch' gables, and perhaps stroll down to St Margaret's (top left), an outstanding late-medieval church, on a rise with a view over the water-meadows to St Mary's, Wiveton (top right).

The water-meadows were open water in the Middle Ages. The long estuary brought ships to the twin ports of Cley and Wiveton, to be drawn up close to where the two churches now stand. The two ports were linked by the late medieval Wiveton Bridge behind trees at the top of the picture.

Cley was an active and prosperous community. By the thirteenth century it had a market, later also four guilds, and its medieval wealth enabled the church to be rebuilt on an impressive scale in the fourteenth and fifteenth centuries. At its height by the sixteenth century, Cley had a good fishing fleet and substantial trade with the Low Countries. Larger ships (some over 100 tons) needed quays and deep water, perhaps forcing a shift northward, nearer to the present town.

In 1612 a 'Great Fire' burnt one hundred and seventeen houses; two which survived, including the Old Hall (extreme left) are late medieval.

However, slow silting of the estuary, followed by the building of the bank across the estuary in 1823 (centre right) confined all trade (now coal, timber, grain and flour) to Cley's north quay; here the windmill, of c. 1800, malthouses and granaries were built. But, the coming of the railway to Holt in 1884 virtually extinguished trade and Cley slowly became a quiet resort.*

Wells-next-the-Sea

TF 916 438 ●▶

The town of Wells is now some considerable distance from the sea itself, as some visitors are surprised to find. It is in fact on the Sluice Creek, which has suffered heavy silting over the centuries. At centre right the channel leading to the sea is paralleled by The Bank, thrown up in 1859 to straighten the channel; the old sea bank can be seen beyond it across a field. Though only small craft are visible in the photograph amongst the salt marshes, quite large vessels do still moor at the quay; not many years ago a storm lifted one up on to the quayside. The town is still subject to flooding in storms; at the end of The Bank, which runs alongside the road down to the sea, are new steel floodgates that can be run across the road.

The street plan consists of a chequerboard layout, with narrow streets often known as 'yards' at right angles to the quay, and others crossing them. The age of this layout is not exactly known; several houses of seventeenth-century origin clearly respect the present street plan. In December 1986 a very unusual timber-framed house of fifteenth-century date was discovered, aligned along one of the yards. However, one house does not make a town plan, and further research is needed on this matter. The church of around 1200, rebuilt in 1450, is at the back of the town (not in photograph) at the head of a once marshy inlet, possibly the site of an earlier harbour, but this point also needs further investigation.

The white building in the left foreground at right angles to the quay is the old Custom House, visited by Samuel Pepys. Beyond it, past the range of nineteenth-century maltings with its gantry and behind the jib of the crane, is the Golden Fleece Inn, a seventeenth-century hostelry with later plaster reliefs, which has welcomed many a weary sailor.*

**Breydon Bridge
Great Yarmouth**

TG 516 080

Great Yarmouth grew up on a sandspit that formed across the mouth of a wide estuary formed by the rivers Yare and Waveney. As the spit extended, the mouth was forced southwards (**93**) and the remains of the tidal estuary dwindled to become Breydon (or 'broadening') Water. This view looks southwards from Breydon down the river towards the sea, with the River Bure entering at centre left and the edge of the old town beyond; to the right are the more recent streets of Cobholm. This topography meant that the town has always been poorly served by roads; for long there was only one bridge, on the site of the present Haven Bridge (top) of the 1920s, the only other land access being over the former sand dunes from Caister-on-Sea. The Acle New Road provided an extra road link in 1831, but the bridging of Breydon was left to the Midland and Great Northern Joint Railway in 1900, when a line was made to connect Yarmouth Beach station with Yarmouth Southtown. After closure of the railway, the superstructure was removed but the piers remained and were used for the construction of the bypass bridge opened in 1986. This is not only a blessing for the town's congested streets but a work of engineering which Norfolk citizens can be proud to bequeath to future generations.*

Great Yarmouth docks

TG 530 039

Great Yarmouth developed on a sandspit between the sea and the river Yare. The South Denes area of the peninsula is on the right-hand side of the picture whilst on the left the town of Gorleston occupies the west bank. Following the gradual decline of the fishing industry in the 1950s, manufacturers were encouraged to locate in the then open area of the South Denes. The power station, seen at the right centre of the picture, was developed in the early 1950s; originally designed for burning coal it was later fired by oil. Large manufacturing companies such as Birds Eye Foods (right background and extreme right foreground of the picture), Hartmann Fibre (right centre), manufacturers of egg cases, and Erie Electronics (right background) now active in the 'high-tech' field, soon followed. The South Denes then became the major manufacturing employment base for Yarmouth. The power station has recently closed, a large part of Birds Eye Foods has re-located out of Great Yarmouth and the large manufacturing companies are owned by multi-nationals and their future is not so certain.

However, from the early 1960s, a re-generation of the area began as the offshore gas industry established itself in Great Yarmouth, initially along the east bank of the river. In the foreground, the Wimpey Marine Base stretches northwards into an area occupied in succession by Conoco and Amoco. Oilrig supply servicing vessels can be seen alongside the quay. The quay was repiled with assistance from the offshore companies from the 1960s onwards and many companies have enjoyed over twenty-one years in occupation. In the centre of the picture the Port and Haven Commissioners' smaller roll-on/roll-off ramp can be seen currently used by a large vessel operating to Esbjerg in Denmark. Further north at the bend of the river is the old fishwharf area where the stone quay has been repiled in steel, thus creating an area where Wood Group Offshore of Aberdeen occupy a large supply base in the Port.

On the west bank of the river the town of Gorleston has developed very close to the quayside, thus restricting port development. This area is occupied by small factory units immediately behind Riverside Road and a number of small inshore fishing craft are berthed alongside the old quay with a new base facility in the left background.

Great Yarmouth harbour mouth TG 533 037 ●▲

As the Yarmouth sandspit grew (91) the exit from Breydon Water was pushed further south, but occasionally storms would force it back to a more northerly position. Eventually it was decided, in the reign of Queen Elizabeth I, to stabilise the harbour mouth in one position, and a scheme of work was devised by a Dutch engineer, known in England as Joash Johnson. This was not completed until 1611. He designed two breakwaters, the North and South Piers, to keep the entrance from silting up; the South Pier (left) was an intricate timber structure which lasted until the 1960s when it had to be replaced in concrete. The Spur Breakwater (top left) prevents the base of the pier being undermined, and the long line of timber fenders within the harbour (to right) keeps shipping in the central channel.

Evidence of the growth of the holiday trade is seen in Gorleston Pavilion (top centre) built by J.W.Cockrill in 1901 in imitation of St Catherine's, Brussels, and important for its early use of terracotta. To the right of the photograph, modern industry spreads over the formerly barren South Denes, which used to be covered with drying fishing nets until the 1950s. The harbour mouth for many years saw the sailing and homecoming of hundreds of herring drifters, which would sometimes fill the river from one side to the other. In recent years shipping serving the oil rigs has replaced the fishing trade (92). Plans have been put forward for a new outer harbour at this point.*

The walled city was the largest in medieval England, larger even than London, with a defensive circuit of some 6.4km including twelve gates. Much of the circuit is now followed by the inner ring road, generally as dual carriage-way, including that section running across the bottom of the picture. The river Wensum (top centre) formed the eastern and part of the northern boundary. The remainder of the northern side is marked in the top left-hand corner where the Victorian terraces start their regular pattern.

Five bridges crossed the river in the Middle Ages. The modern successors of these are visible in the photograph; the only post-medieval bridges are that on the ring road at the extreme left edge, Duke's Palace Bridge, Foundry Bridge and Carrow Bridge off the photograph to the right.

Most of the surviving street pattern is medieval, notable exceptions being Prince of Wales Road, curving from the castle downhill to the railway station, and the dual carriage-way of the inner ring road across the northern part of the historic area.

The earliest parts of the city were probably north of the river, between it and the inner ring road, south of the river in Westwick (close to the ring road bridge) and in the area of the cathedral close. The cathedral (centre) and the castle (below and to the right of the cathedral) are Norman constructions of the eleventh and twelfth centuries, overlying earlier urban occupation. The Normans also developed an open-field site west of the castle as a 'French' borough, centred on the market place and the church of St Peter Mancroft (**95**).*

The first castle at Norwich was probably started in 1067 or 1068 and involved the creation of the great mound or motte (centre) and two enclosures or baileys. The south bailey lies under the car parks to the right of the mound; the north-east bailey is now largely obscured by buildings above and to the left of the mound. The square castle keep on top of the mound dates from about 1100 to 1120 but was re-faced and re-roofed in the nineteenth century. The other buildings on the mound are nineteenth-century prison buildings with some twentieth-century additions for the Castle Museum.

The street alignment of Castle Meadow (at the foot of the mound to its left) follows the line of the castle ditch. To the left of that the curving line of London Street, Castle Street and Back-of-the-Inns marks the edge of the castle fee or 'liberty', the area outside the castle defences but under the jurisdiction of the Crown not the Borough.

The market place was laid out on open fields in the late eleventh century. The church of St Peter Mancroft (right of the market place) was probably founded between 1066 and 1075. The area round the market place was known as Newport ('New Town') or the French Borough as it was originally where the 'Franci de Norvic' or Norman French of Norwich lived.

In recent years there has been considerable large-scale development in the area, starting with the City Hall and its distinctive clock tower in the 1930s. Other developments include the Central Library (bottom, below the car park) and shops on Hay Hill (right of St Peter Mancroft).*

The seat of the bishopric was moved to Norwich from Thetford in 1094. Building of Norwich cathedral began almost immediately and the cathedral church was probably largely complete by 1140. There have been few major changes subsequently, the most important being the replacement of the spire and roofs of the church in the fifteenth century. The rectangular lady chapel at the extreme east end, ruined in the sixteenth century, was rebuilt in the 1930s as a Chapel of Remembrance.

The cathedral was augmented by a Benedictine monastery, remains of which survive to the south, notably the great square cloister. The car park south of the cloister is on the site of the infirmary or monastic hospital while the line of buildings to the east, above the rectangular lawn, stands on the site of the medieval granaries. The bishop had a palace north of the cathedral church, remains of which are now used by the Norwich School (parts can be seen behind the tower).

The close overlies earlier Saxon occupation. It seems likely that numerous roads were cleared to make way for the cathedral and its buildings. One of these roads seems to have run from Whitefriars' Bridge (top right) through the cathedral transepts and out of the close to the south (bottom left), ultimately to join Rose Lane (off the picture). Another, probably Roman, road ran east-to-west from centre right to Tombland, the Late Saxon market place (centre left). Tombland itself was probably rectangular until St George's church and the houses adjacent to it encroached in the post-Conquest period. Houses and churches were either destroyed or incorporated in the close itself. All the churches are now lost, but the site of one of them, St Ethelbert, is likely to be covered by the lawn of Almary Green (centre left, an oval area below the road running from left to right through the close).*

It is difficult to decide which is the more striking in this photograph; the Roman Catholic cathedral or the inner link road. The latter was cut through an area of narrow terraced streets in the 1960s, severing the ancient route along St Giles Street (centre right) to Earlham Road (centre left), now linked only by a footbridge. The site of St Giles's Gates is covered by the road; on the roundabout at bottom right the line of the city wall and a tower is marked by the straight white strip. The new road links with Unthank Road (bottom left), a nineteenth-century development on the land of Colonel Unthank (**99**).

The cathedral of St John the Baptist, standing on the site of the city gaol, was the final crescendo of the Gothic Revival in Norfolk. The creation of the Duke of Norfolk, it was begun in 1884. The architect was George Gilbert Scott junior, who died suddenly in 1897 leaving the east end to be completed by his brother John Oldrid Scott; it was finished in 1910. In the Early English style, it dominates approaches to the town from its high position far more than the medieval cathedral; perhaps it is as well that its proposed spire was never added. Though the Duke intended it as a cathedral from the beginning, it remained an ordinary church until 1976. The only items the Duke left to the congregation to finance were the bells; it has none to this day, and now the tower is too weak through age to support any.

Religious buildings cluster in the cathedral's shadow; the central island building is the Convent of the Little Sisters of the Assumption, centre left is Trinity United Reformed Church, and behind the top of the tower is the Norwich Synagogue.*

The northern suburbs of Norwich were a later growth than those to the west of the city. The right-hand area of the foreground is part of the medieval city, despite the modern appearance of Anglia Square. The line of the city wall is marked by Bull Close Road and Magpie Road (centre right margin to bottom left corner). Beyond Magdalen Gates (centre crossroads) spread Mousehold Heath, barren except for windmills, two leper hospitals, a gibbet and numerous chalk mines. By the late nineteenth century the Heath had been cut back to its present edge at the top of the photograph, and replaced by nurseries, ropewalks, a 'manure factory' and a vast lunatic asylum, by then disused (on the site of Starling Road, bottom left corner). Houses with 'Suffolk White' brick facades went up along the Magdalen Road from the 1880s onwards, the road's ancient route – part of which can be seen as a white track on Mousehold in the background – having earlier been altered and a new road to Sprowston made from Point House, just left of centre. Next, estates in New Catton (left) and New Sprowston (right) were laid out. The right-hand estate of plain red brick houses arose in 1899-1908, with roads named after eighteenth-century politicians. Spencer Street forms a spine road, originally with shops at every crossroads and public houses. The private houses were, however, erected by several different builders, 'bay windows and porches added by prior arrangement'. The chalk mines occasionally try to swallow one. Just below top centre of the photograph, between vacant areas never built over, the George White Middle School is contemporary with the estate. It stands in front of the Start-Rite and Florida shoe factories, a reminder of Norwich's expanding industry at the time.*

Suburbs began to spread on the south-west of Norwich in the parish of Heigham as early as 1810, with the unfortunately named Crook's Place. Colonel C.W.Unthank had a mansion near St Giles's Gates (**97**) with land stretching back towards Eaton, and from 1849 onwards he began to sell off land for housing as working class people began to demand better housing than the crowded courts of the city. The road from the bottom right-hand corner of the photograph to top centre, formerly St Giles's Road, became known as Unthank's Road (now Unthank Road). The streets at top right (in front of the recent Vauxhall Street redevelopment) were the first to be laid out, under strict convenants that for the time were farsighted; white brick had to be used for facades and side walls, roofs were to be slate, unlike the usual pantiles (**98**), gutters were to be iron, and dimensions were controlled – as well as other details such as not allowing washing to be dried in front gardens. The church of Holy Trinity, visible here, was part of the plan (the street is named after it) and was built in 1861 by the architect W.Smith, adding the only pyramid spire to Norwich's skyline. The area, officially known as South Heigham, was popularly called the New City.

At the time of Unthank's death in 1884 these streets were still unfinished. (Those on a different development in the top left of the photograph were at that time being formed). The remaining land was made over to his son, C.W.J.Unthank. The further four streets of the centre section of the photograph are a continuation of the same plan, though the nearer two aligned left to right are a different style of development. The foreground streets at right angles to them are of even more recent date.*

The triangle bounded by Newmarket Road (top left to bottom centre), Ipswich Road (top left to right centre) and Eaton Road (off the picture to the right) has been owned by the Norwich Freemen since 1524 when it was granted to them by Norwich cathedral priory. The Freemen enclosed the eighty-acre triangle with a bank and ditch and it became known as the Town Close.

Freemen grazed their animals on the area until 1701 when the Mayor and Aldermen leased it as a farm to three Norwich butchers, the rent being distributed amongst poor Freemen. In the mid-eighteenth century Jeremiah Ives built the Town Close Mansion, now the Town Close House Preparatory School (building with three chimney pots and adjacent lawn near apex of the triangle).

In 1840 building leases were sold between Town Close House and the tip of the triangle. Further leases were sold in 1852 and included the construction of Town Close Road (linking the Newmarket and Ipswich Roads to the right of Town Close House) and Fairfield and Orwell Roads (either side of the small central triangle). In the late 1860s and early 1870s the estate was developed as far as Lime Tree Road (the road running left of the tennis courts). The spacious elegance of the housing in this area contrasts markedly with that in the two previous pictures.

No further building took place until the 1920s and 1930s when Eaton Road was developed (not in picture). Prior to this Daniels (now Notcutts) Nurseries and the Tennis Club had been established. The triangle was cut by the ring road in 1934 (bottom right running diagonally). Postwar development has seen development off the Ipswich Road and near the ring road in recent years (the curving roads).*

This view of the north-eastern suburbs illustrates a more modern, but similar, piecemeal development to that of the north and west (98-9). Originally all this land was part of Mousehold Heath, but was excluded from the area preserved as a public open space in 1884 (the edge of which appears at centre left). The road crossing the photograph from bottom left to top right is Plumstead Road, and that from bottom right curving to upper left centre is the outer ring road; they cross at the Heartsease roundabout. The foreground roads were within the area known as North Thorpe, partly council housing, laid out from the late 1930s to 1950s. The centre background layout is the Heartsease Estate, with a more complex history. It occupies land formerly a cavalry drill ground, which in 1914 was taken over by the Royal Flying Corps as an airfield. The factories at top left include the original hangars which were served by a tramway laid across Mousehold. In 1927 the field passed to the Norfolk and Norwich Aero Club and in 1932 became Norwich Airport. During World War II it was used as a decoy airfield, and ended its life as a helicopter airmail base in 1950. The city boundary was extended to enclose the area and the housing estate built in the 1960s, including three tower blocks, a rare sight in Norwich. The estate was named from Heartsease Lane and the Heartsease public house at the roundabout – 'heartsease' is an old name for the pansy, but old maps show the pub as The Heart's Ease, perhaps only a name designed to attract custom.

The streets at centre left between Mousehold and Plumstead Road form the Valley Drive estate, private housing built in the 1960s in a huge worked-out gravel pit.*

**Bowthorpe
Development,
Norwich**

TG 182 095 ◄●

The land now occupied by the Bowthorpe Development was purchased by Norwich City Council in 1973, to help meet the city's growing needs for housing land. The 242-hectare site is equivalent to the area within the medieval city walls and is much more than just a housing estate.

In 1974 the Council produced a Master Plan which proposed three 'villages' surrounding a main centre, with additional areas for employment and recreation. Each village would have its own shops, school and village hall while the main centre would meet larger shopping and community needs.

Construction of the first village, Clover Hill, began in 1975, followed by Chapel Break in 1980, with Three Score to come later. In contrast to the Heartsease Estate (**101**) each village consists of a mix of small private, local authority and housing association sites aimed at creating a balanced community of all ages.

The photograph looks east with the main centre in the foreground, with Clover Hill stretching beyond it. Chapel Break is to the bottom left of the picture and the farmland on the right is the edge of Three Score.

At the heart of the development is Bowthorpe Hall and the site of the medieval village of Bowthorpe, of which only the ruins of St Michael's Church remain. These only represent the fourteenth-century chancel; the nave was demolished in the 1630s and the tower by 1790. A new centre for Christian worship, just visible in the bottom right corner of the picture, has been built over the western end of the original church site. Prior to its construction the Norfolk Archaeological Unit excavated the site and revealed evidence that the first church dated back to the eleventh and twelfth century, but finds to the north-west suggest that the settlement itself may date back to the Middle Saxon period.*

The Norfolk Railway was opened in 1845, running from Yarmouth Vauxhall to Norwich, and on to London via Thetford. Its Norwich terminus consisted of a train shed on cast iron columns, and a handsome Italianate office block. The latter was demolished in the 1920s; the former can be seen in this photograph, in the left foreground as the station closest to the river bank, but has since been demolished for a car park. It is hoped the ironwork will be reused in the new Holt station of the North Norfolk Railway. The original maintenance buildings, in the centre of the picture behind the stations, are similarly being cleared away. The company had to be content with this site across the river, although it was inconvenient for access until Prince of Wales Road was cut to connect with it with the city centre in the 1860s.

After the Great Eastern Railway had absorbed the older company, a grand new station in the French Chateau style was designed by John Wilson and erected in 1886 (bottom left). By now it had become known as Thorpe to distinguish it from the Victoria and City stations. Foundry Bridge (bottom left corner) was rebuilt to take the extra road traffic and the Royal Hotel constructed in hope of increased trade. In World War I the light railway to Mousehold Airfield ran from the station forecourt off to the left (**101**).

To the right of the older station can be seen various sidings and depots on the site of the proposed Clarence Harbour (**115**), including a private siding curving inside Boulton and Paul's extensive works where a little yellow engine was a familiar sight, but again alas is no more since the recent closure of this factory. Beyond is Norwich City's Carrow Road football stadium.

In the right-hand corner is King Street. Between the street and the river was the main port area of medieval Norwich, and the quays and warehouses along the river remained busy until this century.*

As rail traffic increased it was found to be inconvenient for holiday expresses from London to Great Yarmouth to have to enter Norwich terminus and wait while the locomotive changed ends. A connecting line, known as the Wensum Curve, was built between the London line (bottom) and the Yarmouth line (top left) to allow through running. Later, a goods yard was laid out alongside. In recent years with the decline in freight traffic and the end of through running to Yarmouth, a new depot has been erected on the site and named Crown Point. The railwaymen however called it the Bermuda Triangle ('Many trains go into it, but none ever come out again'). However, now that its teething troubles are sorted out it handles rolling stock for the London and Birmingham lines and diesel multiple unit servicing for northern East Anglia.

The building with the two chimneys has no connection with the railway, being Norwich's new power station.

In 1881 a new town was founded in Norfolk; the first time this had happened since Norman times (**30-32**). An area of empty land on the borders of the parishes of Melton Constable and Briston was chosen, very near the deserted village of Burgh Parva and its Elizabethan hall whose barns are seen at top right.

The Lynn and Fakenham Railway was extended eastwards to Melton in 1882, and continued on to Norwich City Station. The parliamentary bill for the line was entered for legal reasons in the name of the Norfolk Central Railway and the Eastern and Midland Railway (the small bus shelter at the road junction near the top of the photograph has reused spandrels forming the letters 'NCR'). The Yarmouth and Stalham Light Railway was taken on to Melton in 1883, and the line to Holt from Melton opened in 1884, thus forming the railway crossroads of North Norfolk. The power which now assumed control was the Midland and Great Northern Joint Railway.

The two rows of houses on the left of the main road further from the camera were built first (Melton Street and Astley Terrace) followed by Colville and Briston Roads (left foreground). Those to right of the main road came next. The inhabitants served the railway works (background) and the foremen were given larger houses. A gasworks, water tower, sewage works, school, bowling green, mission hall and pub ('The Hastings Arms') were provided, with a Railway Institute added in 1896. The railway works spawned an early concrete factory. On the station, Lord Hastings, of Melton Constable Hall (**68**), had his own waiting room. All of this still survives except the gasworks – and the railway. Its course can be seen from centre left to top right of the photograph, and a telephone exchange has replaced the station.*

**Great Yarmouth
sea front**

TG 531 070

Yarmouth is a town that faces two ways; the medieval port, tightly packed within the town walls facing westwards to the river and its wharfs (**92**), and the Victorian and later holiday resort shown in this picture, facing east across the North Sea. The tourist industry, which began in the eighteenth century, was to become increasingly important during the nineteenth. By 1759, there was a bath house near the sea front, but it was the coming of the railway which enabled the tourist industry to expand rapidly. By 1854 Yarmouth had achieved 'great celebrity as a bathing place'. Much of the architecture along the front, shown here, dates from this period.

Along the front are several impressive terraces built in the years following 1841 by the Victorian Building Company, 'for the purpose of providing by means of combined capital, large and elegant mansions for the accommodation of the higher class of sea bather'. Kimberley Terrace stands out as a white block beside the road and was described as containing elegant mansions in the Italian style fronted by an esplanade and carriage drive 145 m in length.

The focus of the Edwardian seaside resort was the Parade, stretching from the Britannia Pier (top) to the Wellington Pier (below) at the south. The old jetty between them was originally built in 1560 but replaced in 1809 and used for boat trips. The Britannia Pier, built in 1858, was rebuilt in 1901, but the pavilion burnt down in 1910 and was rebuilt shortly afterwards. The Wellington Pier Company was founded in 1853 and the Pier, with promenades down the length of it, was completed the following year.

The gardens along the front were laid out between 1891 and 1903, the year in which Yarmouth Corporation purchased the Winter Gardens from Torquay and re-erected them adjoining the entrance to the Wellington Pier. This great iron and glass structure which stands out clearly in the photograph was planted with flower beds inside and provided a further seaside attraction, this time under cover.*

Cromer

TG 219 424

Dominating the centre of Cromer is the fine medieval church, reminding us of Cromer's early importance as a fishing village and port for coastal traffic. However, nowadays Cromer is known not only for its crabs, but also as a holiday centre. Its popularity began in the 1780s when it 'was visited by two or three families of retired habits whose favourable reports soon attracted others'. A daily coach from Norwich via Aylsham helped the modest growth of tourism even before the arrival of the railways. Between 1801 and 1851 the town's population doubled.

After 1877, when the railway from Norwich to North Walsham was extended to Cromer, it became easily accessible from London, and the opening of Beach Station by the Midland and Great Northern line in 1892 meant it could be reached from the Midlands as well. Most of the major hotels were built by 1890. The opening of the holiday line meant that at last the Norfolk side of the Great Eastern Railway's operations began to make a profit. The pier was built in 1899 and the lifeboat station added later.

In spite of its seaside attractions, Cromer has never had the funfair atmosphere of Yarmouth and retains its Edwardian charm as a North Norfolk coast holiday resort (**front cover**).*

Mundesley Holiday Centre, Paston TG 320 359

The opening of the Mundesley Holiday Centre in 1933 represented a milestone in the development of the local holiday industry; it was the first purpose-built, fully catering holiday camp in Norfolk and second only to one started in 1930 at Brighstone on the Isle of Wight. They were both the brainchild of Victor Edwards who brought his builder with him from the Isle of Wight. He then went to open a third centre at Kingsdown in Kent. The plan of the Mundesley Centre was intended to reflect the pattern of the sails of a nearby windmill; it was located on an exposed hilltop and therefore looked inwards and not out to sea.

In the early years the central building housed the pump that drew water from an artesian well, and a large diesel engine that generated all electricity for the holiday centre. There were 172 chalets, some in the central cross and the rest around the perimeter; they housed either 1, 2, 3 or 4 people each, and the total capacity of the camp was 360 holidaymakers. All chalets had cold running water laid on but hot water had to be collected from central taps.

The philosophy behind the scheme was to provide a holiday atmosphere totally different from anything people were accustomed to in their ordinary lives. The site was completely self-contained with the social life centred on the ballroom, tennis courts, putting green, croquet lawn, bowls and football, all of which were run by a full-time entertainments organiser. The indoor swimming pool, to the left, was added in 1967.

As other similar holiday camps sprang up around the country, this side of the holiday industry became increasingly competitive. In the 1970s a deliberate decision was therefore taken to concentrate on providing holidays for the over 50s. Nowadays all chalets have hot & cold running water, heating, and private toilets or baths and toilets – all a far cry from what now seem like rather spartan conditions of fifty years ago.

Hemsby Caravan Parks TG 514 148

Until the 1950s most of this was open farmland and, indeed, the farmhouse for Field Farm can be seen to the left. Then, gradually, block by block, the holiday industry took over the area. The first development was the Seabreeze Caravan Park in the left background opened in 1953; the large immaculately-kept Seafield Caravan Park, opposite the farm, followed in 1954. Between the two is the Sunningdale Caravan Park and to the right is the evocatively-named Hawaii Beach Estate of holiday chalets. To the left, and mostly out of the picture, is the Sundowner chalet park complete with sauna and gym with a camping area visible in the foreground. The caravans are mostly individually owned by holiday makers who rent their plots from the site owners.

This is part of a vast complex of holiday homes and holiday camps with clubs, cafes, bingo halls, supermarkets, amusement arcades and a swimming pool, which fits tightly between the village of Hemsby and the sea. Many of the caravan parks and holiday camps are surrounded by their own high wire fences.

In complete contrast to this, nestling in a fold in the sand dunes near the sea is a long row of small Edwardian wooden holiday bungalows. They are built on stilts and have names like Ebb Tide, Skylark and Carbarita. While some have been extended and freshly painted, others stand forlorn and obviously part of a much earlier era in the holiday industry.

The rivers and Broads provide 200 km of lock-free navigation and are particularly well suited for boat cruising. The holiday industry which has grown up around this use is an important part of the economy of the area and provides the opportunity for many thousands of people to enjoy the Broad's waterways. Associated with this holiday industry is a major boat building tradition which is of importance, not just in providing craft for local use, but also for national and international markets.

Potter Heigham is an important centre for both land- and water-borne visitors. The public staithes adjacent to the boatyards shown on the photograph, once used for loading and off-loading produce transported by wherries, still provide rights of access for loading and off-loading boats. Boatyards alongside Potter Heigham Bridge were built largely in the 1920s and 1930s on a scale which anticipated the later expansion that was to occur in boat hiring. Firms attracted government-sponsored expansion and development for small boat building during the Second World War.

The largest complex of sheds, buildings and mooring lagoons were formerly associated with Herbert Woods, nephew of Ernest Woods who pioneered boat building in the Broads with his traditional 'white boat' design. Herbert Woods introduced boat hiring into this area in 1923 and a large hire fleet still operates from this location today. Electric boats operate from the area which is able to claim a 'first' in the introduction of this type of craft onto the Broads.

There has been very little new development in the area in recent years, although this is changing now following permission for a marina to accommodate up to 300 boats. Plans are also in hand to provide an Information and Interpretation Centre, to help the large number of visitors make the most of their holiday on the Broads.

Many people would describe this as a photograph of Wroxham, but in fact most of what can be seen here is Hoveton St John. The left-hand shore is Wroxham – the old village is some distance away – and the bridge is Wroxham Bridge spanning the Bure. It dates from 1619, built on the site of an earlier bridge, and was widened in 1897 when the original stone facing was reset – legend says the stone comes from St Benet's Abbey. It is now concealed from all but boat-people by a modern steel deck, and a footbridge alongside from which visitors can watch cabin cruisers losing their upper projections.

The right-hand bank is Hoveton St John, but again the church is some way away and in the nineteenth century there was only a small group of buildings by the bridge including a watermill, parts of which remain. However, when the railway station was opened in Hoveton it was called Wroxham, and in more recent years the firm of Roys which owns all the large buildings visible used the name Roys of Wroxham, thus compounding the error.

The present size of Hoveton and Wroxham (which extends far beyond what is shown here) dates from the 'discovery' of the Broads as a centre for holidays in the 1920s. The boatyards were dug out and houses built – large and detached at first, but here they have been replaced by more modern residences (bottom right) each with its car parked on one side and its boat moored on the other.*

It is hard for us to imagine the days when scores of windpumps turning their sails were visible across the east Norfolk marshes. Berney Arms is a typical example of the so-called pumping mill, with its encased scoop-wheel for lifting the water from dyke into river Yare, yet originally it was a grinding mill. An earlier mill here did pump water but also ground cement before 1821, and drove a sawmill in later days. The present mill was probably built in 1865, by Stolworth's of Yarmouth. Its seven floors made it the tallest marshmill in east Norfolk, and it was used to grind cement for a works whose footings are visible between the mill and the farmhouse. This closed in 1880 and three years later the mill was converted to drainage, to work until 1948 when the little electric pumphouse beside it took over, the dyke being diverted. The sails on the mill are 'Cubitt's Patent', a type invented by the Norfolk engineer of that name in which the slats can be opened or closed at will. The mill, which takes its name from a nearby wherrymens' inn and has its own railway station, is open to the public and on the Weavers Way footpath.

In the distance can be seen three other windpumps, all ruined, the further two being across the river Waveney in Belton at the foot of the high ground of Lothingland. The area between them is known as Langley Marshes, illustrating how the grazing marsh was divided up into detached portions of outlying parishes.

Ashtree Farm (right) was once known as Five Mile House and up to eighty-nine wherries could be seen resting here at night, their crews tired out after quanting (punting) 8 km upstream from Yarmouth.*

Watermills have a longer pedigree than windmills in this country. At the time of the Domesday survey there were no windmills, but almost any village with a suitable stream had its watermill; Elsing had two. Very often the same site has remained in use and it is probable that this mill occupies one of the Saxon sites, on the Wensum below its junction with Penny Spot Beck. An overflow channel, to take the excess water around the mill when required, is to the right.

The present layout is typical of the Georgian style of watermill; the mill itself with more or less symmetrical facade and central sack hoist in the roof, and to the left the miller's house. These buildings date from 1809 when the establishment was refounded as a paper mill, similar to those upstream at Swanton Morley. By 1845 it had reverted to corn milling and continued to function until recent years.

When the Norfolk Railway Company was constructing its line from Great Yarmouth to Norwich in the early 1840s it encountered difficulties at Thorpe St Andrew. Finding no room between the village and the river on the north bank, it had to erect two bridges; but the city authorities decreed that there must be no obstruction to river traffic. To avoid the nuisance of two opening bridges within a short distance, the railway company dug the New Cut to avoid them. The result was Thorpe Island. The old river (to the left) is still officially part of the City of Norwich – as is all the Yare as far as Hardley Cross – whereas the New Cut, despite now being the main channel, is not within the City's jurisdiction.

By the footbridge in the distance was a tiny halt originally called Thorpe, later Whitlingham. Here took place the infamous and disastrous railway accident in 1874, when the Yarmouth express met the Mail train head on 'with a noise like a clap of thunder' and twenty-five people were killed.

Thorpe St Andrew contains several attractive buildings and is crowded with holiday craft in summer. The church (centre) is of 1866, standing behind the ruins of its predecessor, but its tall spire was removed in 1954. At bottom left the Old Hall is seen under restoration after many years of neglect; it is part of the medieval palace of the Bishops of Norwich, re-made as a house around 1600 by Sir Edward Paston. On the wooded hills behind, some of the Victorian mansions still preserve their grounds amidst the new estates in what was once known as the 'Richmond of Norfolk' because of its river views.

The New Cut, Haddiscoe

TM 455 990

Long before man began to shape the landscape, the rivers wound across it; the Waveney (bottom and right) and in the distance the Yare, both heading for Breydon Water and the sea to the right. Then came the road, from Yarmouth to Haddiscoe (centre). The packhorse and the wherry held sway.

Great Yarmouth controlled the sea trade to Norwich. Why not, reasoned Captain George Nicholls in 1825, build a harbour at Lowestoft, connect it by cuts through Oulton Broad to the Waveney, dig a great new canal from the Waveney to the Yare (the New Cut, centre) and open a grand new Clarence Harbour (**103**) at Norwich? By 1833 this was done...except for the Clarence Harbour, for meanwhile, the railway had been laid from Norwich to Yarmouth. The proposed harbour in Norwich became a railway goods yard and by 1846 the railway had acquired the Cut for a line to Lowestoft and tracks were laid alongside it as if in triumph.

Now the railway ruled. In 1854 the East Suffolk railway company reached Haddiscoe and crossed the older line, to continue northwards to Yarmouth Southtown in 1859. A swing bridge crossed the Waveney (for sail still in theory had right of way) - the stepping-stone-like objects at bottom right are its piers, and the circular object its pivot. The High Level Signalbox to its left is now converted to a house. At bottom left, the curving track and hedges mark a former connection between the two lines.

For now the road had overcome the railway. The East Suffolk line was closed and lifted in 1965, and the New Cut Line has only a limited service. Where a level crossing and swing bridge over the Cut frustrated many car drivers in the 1930s, now a concrete viaduct strides across (centre).

What will this view be like in another hundred years?

Wisbech Canal, Outwell

TF 513 037

'The longest village green in England' as it has recently been described, marks the course of an historic waterway as it runs into the distance between roads in Cambridgeshire (left) and Norfolk (right) surrounded by the typical local scenery of market gardens and greenhouses. It was once the course of the combined rivers Nene and Great Ouse, but the Ouse wandered away to King's Lynn and the Nene was canalised further to the west. At bottom left the Old Nene can still be seen, curving round beyond Outwell church to flow into the Well Creek (bottom right, and **117**).

By 1794 the old river course had been so long dry that houses had been built over it. By Act of Parliament these were demolished to dig out a canal for 8 km reconnecting the Old Nene with the Nene at Wisbech. It was opened two years later. Water was admitted by lock gates at Wisbech – and so was silt, which slowly strangled the canal. Its heyday was in the 1840s, carrying coal to the fenland pumping stations, and passengers to Wisbech by horse-drawn packet. In 1883 the Upwell Tramway was opened alongside (at this point the tramway followed the left hand road) and took away the trade – 600 tons of goods a week (more than the canal carried in a year) and 3,000 passengers. The canal only survived because the local authorities could carry highway materials on it free of charge. In 1926 it was abandoned, though not legally closed until 1939.

Outwell church, in the foreground, has a thirteenth-century tower of stone brought by water from Barnack, near Stamford. The belfry and nave are fourteenth and fifteenth century and the chancel is of 1863.*

Early in the Middle Ages the Great Ouse flowed into the sea north of Wisbech (**116**), but by the middle of the thirteenth century its estuary had become so blocked with silt that the river changed its course to flow eastwards along Well Creek, an artifical channel which had been cut at some earlier date. Well Creek led the waters of the Ouse to Wiggenhall and then to the sea at King's Lynn, and by the fourteenth century it had become such a significant part of the water link between the Midlands and the port of Lynn that attempts to obstruct its course with a dam encountered considerable opposition from merchants and others whose livelihood depended on trade. In 1422 a bank, the New Podike, was constructed close to it to replace the thirteenth-century Old Podike further north which was judged to be beyond repair (**59**).

In 1843 a new drainage scheme involved a long dyke continuing the Cambridgeshire Sixteen Foot Drain, which begins near Chatteris, to the Great Ouse at Wiggenhall. The Middle Level Main Drain, as it was called, had to intersect the Well Creek, and so an aqueduct was provided to carry the Creek over the Drain. (If the reader is confused, all should be clear with the help of an Ordnance Survey map).

The aqueduct, which has since been altered, takes its name from a nearby house, a contraction of St Mary de Bello Loco Court. It occupies the site of a priory possibly founded in Saxon times but reduced to a cell of Ely in 1446 when it was too poor to support even one monk.

Denver Sluice may be called the heart of the Norfolk Fens, not because it is central (it is in fact on the eastern edge) but because all the freshwater arteries meet there. In **118** the river Great Ouse enters at bottom left and winds away into the distance towards the sea, paralleled by the straight cut of the Flood Relief Channel and bridged at the town of Downham Market. At lower right the Cut-Off Channel enters; at centre left the New Bedford River (known more often in Norfolk as the Hundred Foot Drain) appears, and beyond it, here visible only as a narrow white line, the Old Bedford River joins the Ouse at Salters Lode, at the same point as the Well Creek (**117**). (Readers may wish to consult an Ordnance Survey map again at this point).

The Ouse has followed this course since the early Middle Ages when it slowly wandered east from Outwell. The first of the drains was the Old Bedford River, cut by the Dutch engineer Vermuyden in 1637, 33 km from Earith, Cambridgeshire, to Salters Lode to increase the flow of the Ouse by shortening its length; it had 'at each end thereof a Sluice of great strength' of which the northern was 'a great Sasse on Welle Creeke with a stone sluice at Salter's Lode upon Bedford River, to keep out the tides' – the first Denver Sluice. The river was named from the lands drained by the Duke of Bedford. Next came St John's or Downham Eau, a cut on the line of the present Relief Channel in 1642 in order to drain the South Levels into the Lower Ouse. ('Eau' is not here the French for water; properly pronounced 'ee' it comes from the Old English 'ea', river). In 1651 this was greatly extended to the south by the New Bedford River, parallel to the Old Bedford River. Thereafter, the New Bedford took the full flow of the

Ouse and the Old was used only in time of flood; in extreme cases the land between the two, known as the Washes or the Receptacle, could be flooded (25). The actual Ouse was relegated to a backwater south of Denver.

The quality of Vermuyden's system is shown by the fact that it lasted with only minor modifications until 1947. In that year 16,000 hectares of fenland were flooded and it was decided that the drainage system needed modernising. A new drain, prosaically named the Cut-Off Channel, was made from the river Lark at Barton Mills, Suffolk, around the fen edge, intersecting the headwaters of the Upper Lark, Little Ouse and Wissey and the floodwaters from high ground, and carrying them to Denver from where St John's Eau was greatly widened and renamed the Flood Relief Channel.

119 shows the sluices from the other direction. At top right is the sluice on the Great Ouse at its junction with the New Bedford. On the site of one of Vermuyden's sluices to keep the water out of the Old Ouse in 1651, it was rebuilt by Sir John Rennie in 1834 whose fine brickwork remains intact (it is Norfolk's only underwater listed building). It was extended in 1923 and the gates replaced in 1928, 1960 and 1983. The sluice at the centre of the picture on the Relief Channel is part of the 1950s works. To the left smaller sluices control the entry to the Cut-Off Channel. By holding up the outflow and diverting water from the Ouse through the cross channels visible, it is possible to reverse the flow and provide via pipes, tunnels, watercourses and pumping stations, drinking water for Chelmsford and Colchester 150km away.

This pair of photographs illustrates the process by which the salt marshes along the edge of The Wash have been gradually reclaimed for use as farmland. In **120** the series of zig-zag lines indicate the limits of reclamation at different dates; at each stage a new piece of salt marsh was enclosed by a bank and brought under cultivation. In **121** the whole sequence can be seen with the waters of The Wash in the foreground and a freighter from King's Lynn docks heading out to sea. Behind that are the unclaimed

salt marshes, then the sea bank protecting the farmland behind; this in turn changes in the distance to upland and the wooded sandy hills of North Wootton and Castle Rising.

In the foreground of **120** is the Great Ouse, channelled on its way to the sea. Most of the land here was reclaimed this century. The areas to the right in the picture were mostly taken between 1904 and 1928. The central band dates from 1948-50, and the latest intake against the marshes bordering the Wash (top left) ranges from 1955 to 1967.

This plate consists of a pair of vertical photographs taken in 1946, when the airfield was being used as a dump for bombs with nowhere to go. It illustrates perfectly the typical shape of a World War II field in East Anglia with A-plan runways (sometimes called Double X Plan) which allow take-off and landing in any wind direction. Perimeter tracks connect these with the dispersal areas of triangular and circular shape, from which aircraft would join the long procession to the runway. The administration buildings cluster at bottom centre.

It can be seen how the building of the airfield dislocated the locality. From the hamlet of Weston Green in the bottom right angle of the runways the roads running north and west have been cut through, and the left-hand end of the complex bisects another road. Hungate Farm has remarkably been left standing between the main runway and the perimeter track (left of centre); the rectory, in the trees at top right of the field, is surrounded by dispersal areas. The roads have since been restored, but in places the perimeter track has been used instead of the old course.

The base opened in 1941 as a satellite to Swanton Morley, used by 88 squadron who flew the first operational Boston B-3s here. In 1942 it passed to the USAAF 319th bomb wing; 1949 saw their replacement by the 320 (Dutch) squadron. The Americans returned in 1944 with the 466th bomb group who flew 232 combat missions from this field.

In recent years the runways have been used as standings for turkey rearing sheds; several of the original buildings have been retained for agricultural use and the shooting butts still tower over the fields.

This photograph shows an airfield of the same type as Attlebridge (**122**) but where the structures have been removed. Nevertheless the plan is still clear, and even if the runways are totally lifted, the soil disturbance will ensure that it is still visible from the air for years to come.

The base, near to a landing ground used in World War I, was laid out in 1941 between the village and Channonz Hall. It became the home of the U S A A F 445th Heavy Bombardment Group which was active in strategic bombing and in the Battle of the Bulge, flying 282 missions. From 1945 to 1952 it was used as a ferrying centre and Ministry of Food depot. The runways were extended in 1955 as a U S A F standby base. In 1959 it was closed, and was taken over by a gliding club. A former hanger is used for breeding pigeons. The control tower was demolished in 1978.

Disused World War II airfields like this are very much a characteristic feature of the East Anglian landscape.

This photograph shows a combination of features of different dates that at first sight appear baffling, but taken in context illustrate the history of land usage.

Low Farm, centre, stands on the edge of the scattered village of Wood Norton near to the former Norton Moor. The circular black feature beyond it is a marlpit, as in **24**. It is surrounded by ploughing patterns and vehicle tracks.

The jigsaw-like mark across the foreground is a remnant of Foulsham airfield; the perimeter track and two dispersal areas of the type used by bombers. The right-hand area has been returned to agriculture whereas the left-hand area and the track have only had the concrete lifted, hence the difference in appearance. Foulsham was in use from 1942 to 1945, by Mitchells, Lancasters, Wellingtons and Mosquitos and was the scene of the incident in 1944 when a Halifax landed on top of a Mosquito – remarkably without injury to the crews.

The road to the left was cut by the airfield but has been reinstated. The circular marks centre left and right are caused by horse training. The figure-of-eight markings show where horses have been ridden in dressage manoeuvres. The three adjacent circles of decreasing size are where colts have been lunged on the rein, all leaving fascinating patterns on the ground, as are also the two adjoining, snow-filled rings in the nearby field.

Construction of what was RAF Horsham St Faith began in 1939, forming a grass-runway station; the outbreak of war meant that it became operational when still unfinished. Fighter squadrons used the base until June 1940 when Bomber Command took over (it was from this field that Douglas Bader's spare legs were dropped to him at St Omer). In August 1942 Horsham became a USAAF field and in 1943 concrete runways were laid. In 1945 it was returned to RAF Fighter Command and became the centre of many activities – including the dropping of food to swans on Hickling Broad in the winter of 1956 – until its closure in 1963.

The aerodrome then lay dormant until 1967 when Norwich City Council purchased the site and altered the city boundary to include it. It was intended to transform it into the new Norwich Airport, replacing the old Mousehold site (101). The official opening ceremony was held on 30th May 1970. The first jet aircraft to land there had however been a Lightning of 29 Squadron in 1968, the pilot believing it was RAF Coltishall.

The photograph shows the wartime control tower (background) and four of the hangars. The control tower has modern additions and two of the hangars remain in airport use. Other airfield buildings have been converted to a variety of commerial uses, although the building in the bottom right seems to still have camouflage paint on its roof, as do several other buildings in the area.

In recent years the airport has gained a reputation as a convenient link to the Continent; the rebuilding of the terminal building should ensure a continuing growth in trade.

East Dereham
by-pass

TF 995 123

March 20th 1978 was the day peace returned to Dereham. The market town of East Dereham (**80**) owes its size and importance at least in part to its central position in the county and to the fact that it lies astride the main trunk road from Great Yarmouth through Norwich to the Midlands and the North – the A47.

While the post-war boom in motor transport brought the town some of its prosperity – one of its biggest employers is Crane Fruehauf, a leading manufacturer of trailers for articulated lorries – it also brought it misery. By the mid-1970s around 1,200 heavy commercial vehicles and 6,800 cars a day were squeezing through Dereham's narrow streets, blighting the town for residents and drivers alike.

Calls for relief, in the form of a by-pass, started in the fifties and were answered in the spring of 1976 when years of debate about the line of the route culminated in a contract being awarded to build the road which would take the traffic out of Dereham.

The road the Government proposed to build was not to everybody's liking. It was to be for much of its length a single carriageway – not dual as Norfolk had hoped. (Not enough traffic said the Department of Transport). There was even disquiet at the news that it was to be of concrete rather than tarmac.

Nevertheless, there were sighs of relief when the work began and cheers when it was completed nearly two years later – almost 11 km at a cost of nearly £6.5 million – much of it following the line of a disused railway, and giving the motorist the feeling of passing over, rather than through the town.

In **126** the South Green and Toftwood divisions of Crane Fruehauf can be seen either side of the new bypass. To the left the South Green factory, built in 1948, manufactures specialised trailers including military vehicles. To the right the Toftwood factory, built in 1968 alongside the railway line, produces road tankers and tipping semi-trailers.*

County Hall, an eleven-storey building beside the southern section of the outer ring road which encircles the city of Norwich, is the headquarters of Norfolk County Council. The architect was an Australian – Mr Reginald Uren. It was opened on May 24th 1968 by Her Majesty Queen Elizabeth II.

The building brought together for the first time since the inception of the county council in 1888 nearly all its administrative departments, together with the committee rooms and the council chamber in which the councillors make their decisions. Previously the council had met in the Shirehouse in the centre of Norwich and most of its administrative departments were housed in a scatter of buildings at Thorpe Road and elsewhere in Norwich.

The Council and its officers had barely settled into their new home before they were overtaken by another upheaval – the national reorganisation of Local Government in 1974. This swept away the old Rural and Urban District Councils and the County Boroughs and replaced them by seven District Councils and a County Council with responsibility for services in all parts of Norfolk.

Thus, County Hall is now the administrative centre for Education, Social Services, Highways, the Police Force, Planning and the Library Service. The building accommodates some 1,200 of the County Council's 23,000 employees in a setting of 12 hectares of former parkland. The park was designed by Repton around Bracondale Lodge, a Regency house of 1800-20 designed by William Wilkins. The house stood where the steps down from the car park to County Hall now are and it was demolished for the construction of County Hall.It was built for the Martineau family and it later passed to the Colmans.

**South Norfolk
House,
Long Stratton**

TM 194 931

South Norfolk House, the headquarters of the South Norfolk District Council, took advantage of the gravel working of an earlier age, and the trees which it has subsequently sported, to provide a platform and allow the building at eye level to be assimilated into the landscape. Unwilling to be lost in bureaucratic anonymity in Norwich, this District Council chose to site its headquarters at the centre of the predominantly farming district it serves. Designed by Michael Innes of Lambert, Scott and Innes and completed in 1979, the building takes a form which reflects some of the philosophy of the age. Hexagonal in plan and approaching the hemispherical in section, it offers a relative minimum of exposed surface for a maximum of volume enclosed. Coupled with considerable insulation, the form reflects the increasing anxieties and concerns for economy of energy then becoming apparent. The whole of the lower levels form a large flexible office space able to cope with the changing requirements of local government without recourse to building alteration. With an entrance having a sunken rather than a raised emphasis, the intention is to invite rather than to challenge the visitor. Once inside the democracy inherent in the free form of the office is also apparent in the comfortable and accessible reception arena. Banished are images of the 'corridors of power' and the visitor seeks advice in the one place. The roof structures house a somewhat Scandinavian Council Chamber again on an hexagonal plan so that speakers debate more directly towards one another rather than more classically to a platform.

The first sugar beet factory in this country was built at Cantley in the summer and autumn of 1912. The initiative was Dutch and a Mr van Rossum was the main instigator of the project. The scheme was first proposed in 1910 and was revived the following year with the assistance of English colleagues. The company was called The Anglo-Netherlands Sugar Corporation Ltd. and was registered on December 14th 1911. The original factory buildings are clustered around the three tall chimneys at the back of the picture.

The cost of the factory was £170,000 and it operated from 1912 to 1915 at a loss. The company was wound up in 1916 when the assets were acquired by the English Beet Sugar Corporation Ltd. The factory reopened in 1920 and has operated successfully since that date.

In the first season the company processed 21,000 tonnes of beet, the amount now processed every three days. The marshes and lagoon areas of the factory are in effect a wild life preserve and great pains are taken to ensure that the flora and fauna are preserved.

Since 1830 sewage disposal in Norwich has centred on the site at Whitlingham. The sewage was first just pumped onto the surrounding land; then in 1908 the first settlement tanks were installed to trap solids before the rest was spread on the land. Then gradually more treatment facilities were installed as techniques developed. The works now serves the whole of Norwich and many of the surrounding villages. With factory effluents, this represents a population of almost 300,000 people.

The present works, incorporating modern treatment methods, was constructed in two stages. The sixteen circular biological filters (the two banks of eight tanks to the left of the photograph) together with associated primary settlement tanks (to the right of the filters), final settlement tanks (to the left of the filters) and sludge digestors (concrete dome structures) were completed in 1963. Ten years later in 1974 an activated sludge process (the square channelled tank behind the digestors) and four additional final settlement tanks (far centre) were completed.

At the time of its completion, Whitlingham was a world leader, being one of the first sewage treatment works to be computer controlled. Sewage treatment makes use of the biological processes that normally take place in a watercourse and concentrates them into a series of tanks. Sewage is first settled to allow large solids to be removed before being passed to either of the biological treatment processes. These mix tiny, naturally occurring organisms with the sewage impurities and air. The organisms eat and break down these impurities. Final settlement allows the remaining solids to settle as a sludge before the effluent is discharged to the river, having had 90% of the impurity removed. The sludge is kept warm in closed digestors to improve it for disposal onto farmland. The site also houses a laboratory which is equipped for specialist analyses for water, sewage and river services.

The gas terminal stands on the cliffs at Bacton overlooking the North Sea. There are actually three terminals operated by three different companies, Philips, Amoco and Shell, whose sites stretch from the coast road on the left of the picture to the clifftop on the right. On the opposite side of the coast road can be seen part of the terminal operated by British Gas.

The extensive complex of buildings, pipes, storage tanks and equipment results from the discovery in the 1960s of very large reservoirs of natural gas in the rocks beneath the southern North Sea. The north-east coast of Norfolk proved to be the closest landfall for some of the more extensive gas fields, and so a search then began in this part of the county for a suitable site for bringing the gas pipelines ashore. Construction work began at Bacton in 1968.

The three commercial companies now process the gas, extract its impurities, and pass it 'under the road' to British Gas who in turn pass it into the National Grid for use by industry and in homes. The Bacton site was chosen because it was immediately adjacent to the coast, it offers a large relatively flat area of land suitable for building industrial structures, it has reasonably good road access, and is not immediately adjacent to housing (although Bacton village centre is only 1km distant, and holiday caravans may be seen at the bottom of the photograph, separated from the terminal only by one field).

The gas comes from the North Sea drilling platforms (p.32) in 75cm diameter pipes on the sea bed although the pipes are buried in trenches as they approach the coast and pass beneath the beach. The British Gas installation deals with an average of 4,000 million cubic feet of gas per day.

Dates and sources
of the photographs

In the following catalogue, photographs are listed in the order in which they appear in the book; the photographs in the Introductory Sections are numbered by page and those in the main sequence by their numbers.
- The first entry is the page or sequence number.
- The second entry is the date of the photograph.
- The third entry (e.g. NAU) refers to the source and copyright holder of the photograph.
  A list of these abbreviations appears below.
- The fourth entry is the copyright holder's reference. All the photographs were taken by Derek A. Edwards except where otherwise indicated.

Abbreviations used

AAP   Aerial Archaeology Publications, Lansdown House, Breton Close, Toftwood, Dereham, Norfolk NR19 1JH

AC   Allen Collection: Ashmolean Museum, Oxford OX1 2PH

CUCAP   University of Cambridge Committee for Aerial Photography, The Mond Building, Free School Lane, Cambridge CB2 3RF

NAU   Norfolk Archaeological Unit, Union House, Gressenhall, Dereham, Norfolk NR20 4DR

NNFC   Aerial photography of the former Norfolk & Norwich Aero Club Ltd: © Aerial Archaeology Publications, Lansdown House, Breton Close, Toftwood, Dereham, Norfolk NR19 1JH

RAF   Royal Air Force

RCHME   Crawford Collection: Royal Commission on the Historical Monuments of England, National Monuments Record - Aerial Photographs, National Monuments Record Centre, Kemble Drive, Swindon, Wiltshire SN2 2GZ

SAU   Suffolk Archaeological Unit, Shire Hall, Bury St Edmunds, Suffolk IP33 2AR

Cover illustrations

front 11 Jul 86 NAU TG2142/K/DDN1
back 15 Jun 86 NAU TF8114/ACH/DDR6

Introduction

p8 5 Feb 46 RAF 3G TUD.UK59.PartIV. 5Feb46.F.12'//90Sqdn frame 5132 (Photo by Royal Air Force)
p11 2 Jul 77 NAU TF9819/AFY/AHN23

Illustrations

1 5 Aug 77 NAU TF7425/C/ALT3
2 2 Mar 86 NAU TG0242/J/AZR27
3 15 Jul 86 NAU TF6742/C/DDU8
4 15 Apr 83 NAU TG2639/C/ASQ7
5 4 Aug 77 AAP 138/13/(Photo by E.A. Horne)
6 27 Apr 84 NAU TM3491/Q/AXE9
7 31 Jul 77 NAU TG2235/F/AKP24
8 9 Jun 80 NAU TG2306/E/ANU5
9 2 Apr 84 NAU TL8189/R/AUM18
10 30 Jul 77 NAU TG3019/D/AKH7
11 16 Jul 84 NAU TM3493/AP/AXH16
12 24 Jun 76 NAU TF9440/V/AEP13
13 13 Jul 80 NAU TF8435/AM/APT14
14 25 May 78 AAP 161/18 (Photo by E.A. Horne)
15 30 Jun 82 NAU TL8782/X/ARW20

16 30 May 80 SAU ALD3 (Photo R.D. Carr)
17 24 Jul 82 NAU TL8685/ABS/ARU15
18 17 Jun 74 NAU TG2519/X/AAZ44
19 16 Jul 86 NAU TG1424/A/DBL11
20 16 Jul 84 NAU TG4704/AFT/AXK6
21 4 Jul 74 NAU TF7844/G/AAE12
22 24 Jul 28 RCHME 2322 (Photo by Royal Air Force)
23 1 Jul 76 NAU TG2223/ACX/AFF11
24 15 Jul 80 NAU TF7333/A/AQB14
25 5 Jun 37 AC 1335 (Photo by Major G.W.G. Allen)
26 8 Jul 76 NAU TF5700/H/AFX1
27 19 Jul 77 NAU TF9819/AGN/AJC15
28 30 Jun 78 AAP 167/14
29 1933-8 NNFC No Reference (Photo by Norfolk & Norwich Aero Club)
30 27 Jul 76 NAU TF8115/ABA/AGS6
31 28 Jul 83 NAU TF6624/ABB/ATJ25
32 29 Jun 76 NAU TM0890/D/AEY12
33 15 Apr 83 NAU TF9839/V/ASQ9
34 8 Jul 76 NAU TF6600/A/AFW12
35 27 Jul 79 AAP 194/15 (Photo by E.A. Horne)
36 29 Jul 83 NAU TG3815/Y/ATN11
37 10 Jul 85 NAU TF9336/AL/AZA5
38 9 Feb 84 NAU TM0294/A/ATW1
39 24 Jun 76 NAU TF7222/W/AES9
40 21 Jan 67 CUCAP AQS45 (Photo by Professor J.K.S. St Joseph)
41 9 Aug 77 NAU TF9022/S/ALX17
42 1 Jun 62 CUCAP AEX10 (Photo by Professor J.K.S. St Joseph)
43 26 Nov 60 CUCAP AAQ50 (Photo by Professor J.K.S. St Joseph)
44 27 Apr 84 NAU TM2292/D/AXA26
45 5 Feb 84 NAU TM0691/B/ATS2
46 16 Jul 86 NAU TG1218/D/DBK9
47 5 Feb 84 NAU TM1198/A/ATT3
48 27 Apr 84 NAU TM2398/S/AWZ14
49 27 Apr 84 NAU TM2499/C/AWZ27
50 3 Mar 86 NAU TF9821/ABX/AZM3
51 27 Apr 84 NAU TM1582/A/AWP18
52 15 Apr 83 NAU TG1124/J/ASM13
53 26 Mar 85 NAU TM1685/E/AYF12
54 16 Jul 86 NAU TG1530/A/DBM8
55 29 Jun 76 CUCAP BYJ29 (Photo by Professor J.K.S. St Joseph)
56 15 Jan 75 CUCAP BRX103 (Photo by D.R. Wilson)
57 1 Aug 86 NAU TM1797/A/DDD9
58 11 Jun 52 CUCAP H183 (Crown Copyright Reserved)
59 9 Feb 84 NAU TF5505/B/AUB23
60 30 Mar 83 NAU TG1238/Q/ASJ27
61 23 Jul 85 NAU TF7401/AB/AZC18
62 27 Apr 84 NAU TM3696/V/AXD16
63 15 Apr 83 NAU TG1432/C/ASN12
64 25 Feb 76 NAU TF9033/K/AEA28
65 3 Aug 76 NAU TG1728/G/AGU4
66 17 Apr 84 NAU TF7928/F/AVE1
67 3 Mar 86 NAU TF7927/G/AZM19
68 4 Apr 84 NAU TG0331/S/AUX18
69 15 Apr 77 AAP 110/23
70 27 Apr 84 NAU TM0387/F/AWT13
71 30 Mar 83 NAU TG0316/S/ASF12
72 4 Apr 84 NAU TG0318/S/AUW1

73 10 Jul 85 NAU TF6928/B/AYY18
74 27 Apr 84 NAU TM1187/E/AWS9
75 15 Apr 83 NAU TG4326/A/ASP21
76 4 Apr 84 NAU TF8836/AP/AYB20
77 4 Apr 84 NAU TF9040/B/AVA17
78 30 Mar 83 NAU TF9717/T/ASF7
79 26 Mar 85 NAU TM1887/G/AYF16
80 10 Jul 85 NAU TF9813/AF/AYW5
81 12 Jul 74 NAU TF8209/B/ADB17
82 10 Jul 85 NAU TF8342/Q/AYZ19
83 27 Apr 84 NAU TM1179/F/AWQ24
84 30 Jun 82 NAU TL8683/V/ARW19
85 10 Jul 85 NAU TF6120/L/AYW17
86 10 Jul 85 NAU TF6120/P/AYW20
87 10 Jul 85 NAU TF6120/U/AYW25
88 10 Jul 85 NAU TF7944/D/AYZ4
89 10 Jul 86 NAU TG0444/A/DAW17
90 4 Apr 84 NAU TF9143/K/AUY27
91 8 Jul 85 NAU TG5108/L/AYR18
92 8 Jul 85 NAU TG5303/Q/AYS7
93 8 Jul 85 NAU TG5303/R/AYS8
94 11 Nov 85 NAU TG2308/ABB/ASA24
95 8 Jul 85 NAU TG2208/L/AYQ27
96 8 Jul 85 NAU TG2308/AG/AYP14
97 8 Jul 85 NAU TG2208/D/AYP22
98 18 Aug 86 NAU TG2309/ABL/DEJ13
99 18 Aug 86 NAU TG2107/A/DEJ9
100 18 Aug 86 NAU TG2207/L/DEJ8
101 11 Nov 85 NAU TG2509/A/ASA20
102 18 Aug 86 NAU TG1809/Q/DEC16
103 8 Jul 85 NAU TG2308/AU/AYQ23
104 8 Jul 85 NAU TG2407/J/AYQ13
105 30 Mar 83 NAU TG0433/J/ASH14
106 8 Jul 85 NAU TG5307/C/AYS11
107 8 Jul 85 NAU TG2142/D/AYT18
108 2 Mar 86 NAU TG3235/B/AZR7
109 29 Jul 86 NAU TG5114/F/DEC9
110 29 Jul 83 NAU TG4118/C/ATQ10
111 17 Jul 84 NAU TG3018/A/AXM13
112 8 Jul 85 NAU TG4604/C/AYR3
113 30 Mar 83 NAU TG0517/U/ASG6
114 11 Jul 86 NAU TG2508/Q/DBA4
115 29 Jul 86 NAU TM4599/N/DCY1
116 23 Jun 85 NAU TF5103/H/AZG8
117 23 Jul 85 NAU TF5302/E/AZG2
118 18 Jul 86 NAU TF5800/G/DCC3
119 23 Jul 85 NAU TF5801/K/AZF22
120 23 Jul 85 NAU TF6124/B/AZH7
121 10 Jul 85 NAU TF6026/A/AYW26
122 30 Mar 46 RAF 3G TUD.UK100.Part IV.
30Mar46.F.12'//90Sqdn frames 5322 and 5323
(Photos by Royal Air Force)
123 26 Mar 85 NAU TM1488/F/AYF5
124 9 Dec 80 NAU TG0227/B/AQP3
125 20 Feb 87 NAU TG2213/D/DEL20
126 29 Jun 76 NAU TF9912/B/AFB7
127 10 Jul 85 NAU TF9912/E/AYW11
128 8 Jul 85 NAU TG2407/F/AYQ10
129 31 Jul 84 NAU TM1993/C/AXW2
130 30 Jun 86 NAU TG3808/G/DAR25
131 11 Jul 86 NAU TG2707/E/DBA20
132 8 Jul 85 NAU TG3334/D/AYT4

Suggestions for Further Reading

Norfolk

Clarke, R.R., (1975) *East Anglia*, Wakefield, EP Publishing

Darby, H.C., (1983) *The Changing Fenland*, Cambridge, Cambridge University Press

Darroch, E. and Taylor, B., (1975) *A Bibliography of Norfolk History*, Norwich, University of East Anglia

Dymond, D., (1985) *The Norfolk Landscape*, London, Hodder & Stoughton

East Anglian Archaeology 1 (1975 onwards)

Harrod, W. and Linnell, C.L.S., (1966) *Norfolk*, London, Faber & Faber

Martins, S.W., (1984) *A History of Norfolk*, Chichester, Phillimore

Pevsner, N., (1973) *The Buildings of England: North-West and South Norfolk*, Harmondsworth, Penguin Books

Pevsner, N., (1976) *The Buildings of England: North-East Norfolk and Norwich*, Harmondsworth, Penguin Books

Ravensdale, J. and Muir, R., (1984) *East Anglian Landscapes*, London, Michael Joseph

Wade-Martins, P., (1993) *Historical Atlas of Norfolk*, Norwich, Norfolk Museums Service

Williamson, T., (1993) *The Origins of Norfolk*, Manchester, Manchester University Press

Winckley, G., (1986) *The Country Houses of Norfolk*, Lowestoft, Tyndale and Panda Publishing

Yaxley, D., (1977) *Portrait of Norfolk*, London, Robert Hale

Air Photography

Aerial Archaeology 1 (1977 onwards), Dereham, Aerial Archaeology Publications

Beresford, M.G.W. and St Joseph, J.K.S., (1979) *Medieval England: an Aerial Survey*, Cambridge, Cambridge University Press

Bradford, J., (1974) *Ancient Landscapes: Studies in Field Archaeology*, London, Greenwood Press

Deuel, L., (1969) *Flights into Yesterday*, London, MacDonald

Frere, S.S. and St Joseph, J.K.S., (1983) *Roman Britain from the Air*, Cambridge, Cambridge University Press

Hudson, K., (1984) *Industrial History from the Air*, Cambridge, Cambridge University Press

Muir, R., (1983) *History from the Air*, London, Michael Joseph

Platt, C., (1984) *Medieval Archaeology from the Air*, London, Guild Publishing

Riley, D.N., (1982) *Aerial Archaeology in Britain*, Princes Risborough, Shire Publications Ltd

St Joseph, J.K.S., (1977) *The Uses of Air Photography*, London, John Baker

Wilson, D.R., (1982) *Air Photo Interpretation for Archaeologists*, London, Batsford

Index of place names

This index refers to places illustrated or mentioned in the text.
- Bold figures refer to the sequence of photographs.
- Italic figures indicate the page number of an illustration in the Introduction.
- Other figures indicate a text reference in the sequence of photographs unless prefixed 'p' which indicates a page number in the Introduction.